A Pool of Reflections

*for the refreshment of travellers on
the Spiritual Path*

by

RAYNOR C. JOHNSON

HODDER AND STOUGHTON
LONDON SYDNEY AUCKLAND TORONTO

229

To MARY
GOOD COMPANION and LOYAL FRIEND
COMMEMORATING
FIFTY YEARS

Author's Preface

THE STRANGE PILGRIMAGE OF HUMAN LIFE HAS ITS UNIQUENESS FOR each traveller. This is why that rare communion in depth with fellow-travellers can be sometimes very moving and enriching. The journey which we are all making has its 'green pastures and still waters' of tranquillity, its hills of difficulty, its mountain-peaks of vision and inspiration, its gloomy valleys of sorrow and perplexity, and its dry deserts of emptiness. When by our own choice the long travel of many lives leads us on to the Spiritual Path, we know that the Journey's end is drawing near. Like the Prodigal, we are on the way Home. All other paths must at some point lead in to this one and then the intellect has fulfilled its principal task and the heart must become the pilgrim's compass.

I have gathered together a few reflections from the surface of a quiet lake in a dark valley through which I travelled before leaving it behind. The sensitive insights of many poets have helped me to capture these reflections more than prose could ever hope to do, – and perhaps the reader will give thanks to the Great Poet and Artist, as I have often done.

Rupert Brooke wrote at the age of twenty (and eight years later he finished his brief life):

> O Thou,
> God of all long desirous roaming,
> Our hearts are sick of fruitless homing,
> And crying after lost desire.
> Hearten us onward! as with fire
> Consuming dreams of other bliss.

The best Thou givest, giving this
Sufficient thing – to travel still
Over the plain, beyond the hill,
Unhesitating through the shade,
Amid the silence unafraid,
Till at some sudden turn, one sees
Against the black and muttering trees
Thine altar, wonderfully white,
Among the Forests of the Night.

RAYNOR C. JOHNSON

Acknowledgments

GRATEFUL ACKNOWLEDGMENT IS MADE TO THE FOLLOWING PERSONS or firms for their permission to use copyright material. Every effort has been made to trace the owners of copyright for permission and if there has been any failure in this the author asks for indulgence.

To Jonathan Cape Ltd for a poem from *The Collected Poems of W. H. Davies*, and a poem of Muriel Stuart; to Messrs. Chapman & Hall Ltd for extracts from Allen Brockington's book *Mysticism and Poetry*; to Gerald Duckworth & Co Ltd for a poem from Charlotte Mew's *Collected Poems*; to Messrs. Victor Gollancz Ltd for extracts from *A Drug-Taker's Notes* by R. H. Ward; to Messrs. George Harrap & Co Ltd for two poems of William Watson; to Messrs. A. M. Heath & Co Ltd for extracts from *The Selected Poems of A. E.* (George Russell), two extracts from *The Avatars, and Imaginations and Reveries*, published by Macmillan & Co, with acknowledgments also to Mr Diarmuid Russell; Messrs. Hollis & Carter who published the Centenary edition in 1947 of *The Poems of Alice Meynell*: to Messrs. Hodder & Stoughton Ltd for a poem taken from *The Unutterable Beauty* by G. Studdert-Kennedy; the Hutchinson Publishing Group Ltd for extracts from *The Teachings of Ramana Maharshio* by Arthur Osborne, and from *Grades of Significance* by G. N. M. Tyrrell; to Mrs Celia Kendon for a poem of her late husband Frank Kendon; the Longman Group Ltd for an extract from *Grey of Fallodon* by G. M. Trevelyan, and a poem of Eva Gore-Booth; to Sri K. Sankara Menon for permission to use several poems of the late Dr James H. Cousins published by Messrs. Kalakshetra of Adyar, India; to Messrs. Macmillan & Co of

London and Basingstoke for extracts from *Poems of the Unknown Way* by S. R. Lysaght, and a poem of T. E. Brown; to Penguin Books Ltd for an extract from the *Bhagavad Gita* trs. by Juan Mascaro; to Messrs. Routledge & Kegan Paul Ltd for three extracts from *The Secret of the Golden Flower* being part of Jung's commentary; Sri Ramakrishna Math of Mylapore, Madras, for extracts from the Sayings of Sri Ramakrishna; to Charles Scribner's Sons for extracts from *Music and Other Poems* and from *The Builders and Other Poems* both by Henry Van Dyke; to Messrs. Sidgwick and Jackson Ltd for extracts from *The Collected Poems of Rupert Brooke*; to Messrs. Visva Bharati of Calcutta for extracts from Letters to a Friend by R. Tagore, ed by C. F. Andrews; to Messrs. A. P. Watt & Son for an extract from *The Collected Poems of W. B. Yeats* by permission of M. B. Yeats and Macmillan companies of London and Basingstoke, and Canada, also an extract from a novel *The Glimpse* by Arnold Bennett by kind permission also of Mrs Dorothy Bennett; to Messrs. Neville Spearman for an extract from *Post-Mortem Journal* by Jane Sherwood; to Messrs. Methuen & Co Ltd and Clement Shorter for a poem by Dora Sigerson; and to Mr. Henry Bryan Binns for his poem *Advent*.

R. C. J.

Contents

1

What Then?

YOU ARE SITTING IN A CHAIR READING THIS BOOK, OR LISTENING
to it being read. Why are you doing so? Do not accept as satis-
factory the first answer that comes but probe as deeply as
possible. Every answer may cover up a deeper question, and
if you are relentless you will finally arrive at some question
which involves your search for truth. You will also find a pro-
visional answer to it that you have acted upon in choosing your
path through life although you may not consciously have
formulated this in words.

The basic question can be put in various forms, but they
amount to the same thing. What am I doing here on earth? Why
was I born to particular parents at a particular time? Why
have I to face my particular life-situation, which is different
from others? Is this chance or accident, or has it some ultimate
meaning? If it has meaning, how can I find the clues? Am I
using my life wisely or otherwise? When this life of mine draws
to its close: "What then?"

W. B. Yeats wrote some verses, not, I think, very memorable
as poetry, but nevertheless inviting the ordinary man to look
at his accepted values.

> His chosen comrades thought at school
> He must grow a famous man;
> He thought the same and lived by rule,
> All his twenties crammed with toil;
> "What then?" sang Plato's ghost, "What then?"

Everything he wrote was read,
After certain years he won
Sufficient money for his need,
Friends that have been friends indeed;
 "What then?" sang Plato's ghost, "What then?"

All his happier dreams came true –
A small old house, wife, daughter, son,
Grounds where plum and cabbage grew,
Poets and Wits about him drew;
 "What then?" sang Plato's ghost, "What then?"

"The work is done", grown old he thought,
"According to my boyish plan;
Let the fools rage, I swerved in naught,
Something to perfection brought";
 But louder sang that ghost, "What then?"

In our Western setting with its cultural and educational background, we have an extraordinarily casual attitude to human life. We don't pretend to know what human life means, nor are we (with exceptions) much concerned to find out. We are born into a particular family with something which we call our character or disposition. We do not enquire where it has come from. It may harmonise or clash with those around us. It can be modified in some degree, and in its turn, it can modify that of others. We adopt a code, although we may seldom attempt to express it in words. We finally leave the family background and start to contend with a world that is generally hard or indifferent to our success or our failure. We call this fight with our environment "ambition", "business", "duty", "the rat race", or "making a contribution to society" according to our disposition. If, as is frequently the case, our daily work offers satisfaction to only one side of our nature, we turn in our spare time to interests that will remedy this. Perhaps we form personal attachments that will assuage our loneliness or isolation. We may look for pleasure that will offer a contrast to the daily treadmill. We may take an interest in arts that will lift us out of the harsh commonplaces of life and unveil to us a world of beauty and imagination. Inevitably changes come, and we meet disappointment and disillusionment. We are "let down" and we suffer. Life is not what we hoped it might become. We emerge from some dark patches never quite the same person again. Perhaps we build a protective shell around us so that in future we shall not be hurt so much. So we live and love, adapting and adjusting, making the best of it, dreaming our dreams, following our routine, paying the price demanded by our society for what is called pleasure or satisfaction. In this way, the years pass for the majority of people. We make our mistakes; we hope we are learning from them, and we imagine that somehow, somewhere, beyond the conscious part of our being, there may be a little treasury of experience or wisdom that is slowly growing.

But to what end is all this tending? What goal have we in mind just over the horizon? What men call birth and death are mysteries towards which our mental questioning is occasionally directed: but what do we *know*? Most men ignore the horizons and decide to live in the present for the present. Now and again the deeper questions return to haunt us.

> But O to know not while with friends I sit,
>   And when the purple joy is passed about,
> Whether 'tis ampler day divinelier lit
>   Or homeless night without.

They return to haunt us most keenly when someone whom we dearly love passes on. The physical form with which we have identified him or her is no longer with us. Is this the end? Plato's ghost would say "What then?" Surely we should be able to find *certainty* and not have to fall back on faith or hope in regard to matters which are of supreme importance to us? To this question I answer "It is quite possible to have certainty". But since this absolute knowledge is mystical, i.e., knowledge held by the soul, not by the intellect; the certainty, while absolute for its possessor, is only second-hand when it is expressed in words and handed on to another. Because I am writing from my heart I can only record the truth which my soul knows – and to it my heart responds joyfully. (My mind has strong supporting evidence, but this does not concern me here.)

I, my true Self, my Soul, has always been and always will be – because God loves me. What God loves can never perish or be lost for it is precious to Him. So great indeed is this Love, that in His compassion for us we are shielded from the direct beams.

Aeons ago, all the souls now incarnate in bodies or vehicles exercised the freewill which had been given to them and left the immediate presence of their Creator. Of their own volition they undertook the age-long process of descent through realm after realm of diminishing reality. In the course of this process souls acquired numerous bodies which became instruments allowing them to operate on these levels. They fulfilled their purpose but became in so doing the soul's prison-house. Each incarnate soul is now a prisoner of the lowest level of descent, the realm we call the physical world. When the physical body dies, an individual finds himself in an astral body on one of the many attractive "astral" levels. (These are called heaven-worlds by most of the religions.) They are only a few steps up-ward towards reality. They are Camp I, as it were on the spiritual Everest which beckons souls upward. The ability to climb to higher camps depends upon the degree of spiritual acclimat-isation which a soul has won for itself while here on earth. Most souls find it necessary to reincarnate very many times on to the physical level, before they are able after physical death to climb higher. Herein lies the importance of using rightly the opportunity offered to us when we re-acquire a physical body.

What is meant by "spiritual acclimatisation"? The first step for each incarnate individual is to awaken to the true state of affairs. Such an awakening came to the prodigal son in the "far country" (which symbolises the earth). This famous parable relates that at long last a great famine arose and he began to be in want. When he had suffered enough, he remembered some-thing he had long forgotten, his Father's House, and he decided to set off on the long journey back. We are not told much of this journey except that at a certain point on his return he was met by his Father, who had been on the look-out, and saw him coming from afar. The Father, says the parable, "ran to meet him, fell on his neck and kissed him". True Love, the divine love of the Father is timeless, therefore changeless and eternal. It had suffered with and for the one who suffered. There was no judgment of him, no criticism of any kind, – there was only the most loving welcome. We judge and condemn ourselves. A great Master once said, "There is no sorrow quite like that which arises when you see one you love going into self-inflicted darkness."

Our human love may change and fail, but of divine love it has been said,

> ... the love of God is broader
>   Than the measures of man's mind,
> And the heart of the Eternal
>   Is most wonderfully kind.

The return journey is the greatest and most difficult journey we can undertake. It first requires the sleeper to awaken from the illusions of human life in the far country of earth. Have we awakened and taken the first steps?

2

The Hound of Heaven (i)

THIS LENGTHY POEM OF FRANCIS THOMPSON RANKS FOR ME, WITH
Wordsworth's *Ode on Intimations of Immortality* among the half
dozen greatest poems in the English language. Thompson died
at the early age of forty-eight in 1907. His father had wanted
him to follow his own profession, that of medicine – but he had
no feeling for this as a vocation and as a consequence failed in
the necessary examinations. Saddened by his father's attitude
he reluctantly decided to leave Manchester, with the gloomiest
of forebodings, and try to find some work that he could do in
London. As time passed he gradually found himself without
adequate means of support, sleeping in common doss-houses
on the Thames embankment, and living among the poorest of
the poor. There was one poignant episode of this sad period of
his life, which is worth relating. He was found one night by a
girl of the streets who saw that he was famished, and out of the
kindness of her heart took him to her humble room and shared
with him her meagre resources. He treated her with respect and
love, an attitude which she had not known hitherto. About
this time, Wilfrid and Alice Meynell who later became his
sponsors and benefactors, were trying to trace the young poet.
The girl heard of this, and realising that it was the beginning of
a widening opportunity for him, begged him to leave her. She
said to him, "I always knew you were a genius. Please leave me
now. They will not understand." Thompson refused, and the
girl, seeing it was useless to try to persuade him, disappeared
one night and never returned. Although in his misery he looked
for her for years in haunts that were familiar to them both, he
never found her again . . . Of how the Meynells found him,

nourished him, and encouraged his genius is well known. He had unhappily acquired a measure of addiction to opium smoking to which he had been introduced by de Quincey and his mother. This addiction, together with an enfeebled constitution probably arising from the period of under-nourishment led finally to T.B. from which he died at forty-eight in a London hospital. The mystical traditions of the Roman Catholic Church, of which he became a member, appealed to him, and at many points his poetry bears the imprint of this devotion. Meredith said of his genius that he was "a true poet – one of a small band". Wilfrid Meynell paid tribute to him in these memorable words: "Devoted friends lament him, no less for himself than for his singing. Let none be named the benefactor of him who gave to all more than any could give to him. He made all men his debtors, leaving to those who loved him the memory of his personality, and to English poetry an imperishable name."

The Hound of Heaven has one theme: God's unwavering pursuit of the soul of man, and man's persistent effort to escape from "this tremendous Lover".

> I fled Him, down the nights and down the days;
>   I fled Him, down the arches of the years;
> I fled Him, down the labyrinthine ways
>   Of my own mind; and in the mist of tears
> I hid from Him, and under running laughter.
>   Up vistaed hopes I sped;
>   And shot, precipitated
> Adown Titanic glooms of chasmèd fears,
>   From those strong Feet that followed, followed after.
>   But with unhurrying chase,
>   And unperturbèd pace,
>   Deliberate speed, majestic instancy,
>   They beat – and a Voice beat
>   More instant than the Feet –
> "All things betray thee, who betrayest Me."

The poet reminds us that we can use intellect as a hide-out from God. Sages have told us that the mind is the enemy of the Real, and that words and concepts, beliefs and creeds, arguments and philosophies – the "labyrinthine ways of the mind" –

may become smoke-screens and clouds which obscure from us the ever-shining sun of the Real. Equally, we may hide in the "mist of tears", in emotions and in self-pity from the Divine Lover. This is a more subtle withdrawal, for there is something about grief and suffering which tends to make the sufferer draw into himself, feeling that no-one else can quite understand or share his loneliness. The Divine Lover alone does understand perfectly, but it is a human reaction to feel that no-one can.

The fugitive then seeks to find some comfort in friendship and human companionship:

> I pleaded outlaw-wise,
> By many a hearted casement, curtained red,
> Trellised with intertwining charities;
> (For, though I knew His love Who followèd,
> Yet was I sore adread
> Lest, having Him, I must have naught beside)
> But, if one little casement parted wide,
> The gust of His approach would clash it to.
> Fear wist not to evade, as Love wist to pursue.

It is a strange human misapprehension, yet not an uncommon one, that the Love of God for the soul of man must rule out every other love. This has led at times to asceticism and monasticism, to celibacy and solitude, and these may play their part in a man's development. If these are God's final call to man they are difficult to reconcile with the life and spirit of Jesus Who saw a world in which His Father was always present and working, and Who gave to His disciples a paramount commandment "that ye love one another as I have loved you". God asks for our love without reserve, but He gives back to us far more than we can ever give to Him. I recall once meditating on the Love of God, and receiving a clear message from some higher level: "Love Me first, fully, and unconditionally: all other loves are My gifts to you." It is as though the great sun of love irradiates all space with its beams, but here and there are souls who are like mirrors placed at the correct angle, each one reflecting back to us something of the sun's brightness. If the little "casements" are closed to us it must surely be to avoid our resting in a false security.

The fugitive then seeks refuge in aestheticism, but this leads to the confession:

> I tempted all His servitors, but to find
> My own betrayal in their constancy,
> In faith to Him their fickleness to me . . .

It is no good seeking to make the decorations of the house of life a substitute for interior soundness; to suppose that artistic sophistication can be a substitute for a kind unselfish nature! The good may be the enemy of the best, and may draw men back from high levels of consciousness to face again in a physical body the enduring simplicity of being very true and very loving.

The fleeing soul then seeks in excitement and speed forms of escape, but the Divine Feet maintain their pursuit and the Voice says:

> "Naught shelters thee, who wilt not shelter Me."

He then turns to childhood, perhaps to family life, for comfort.

> I sought no more that after which I strayed,
>   In face of man or maid;
> But still within the little children's eyes
>   Seems something, something that replies,
> *They* at least are for me, surely for me!
> I turned me to them very wistfully;
> But just as their young eyes grew sudden fair
>   With dawning answers there,
> Their angel plucked them from me by the hair.

Then the fugitive turns to Nature to find a fellowship which human kind had failed to offer him. He seeks also an understanding of Nature's laws. He speaks of how he "drew the bolt of Nature's secrecies", and says:

> I triumphed and I saddened with all weather,
>   Heaven and I wept together,
> And its sweet tears were salt with mortal mine;
> Against the red throb of its sunset heart

> I laid my own to beat,
>   And share commingling heat;
> But not by that, by that, was eased my human smart.
> In vain my tears were wet on Heaven's grey cheek.
> For ah! we know not what each other says,
>   These things and I; in sound *I* speak –
> *Their* sound is but their stir, they speak by silences.

At last he discovers that Nature cannot meet his deepest needs.
The pursuing Feet move closer and closer to him

> Nigh and nigh draws the chase,
>   With unperturbèd pace
> Deliberate speed, majestic instancy;
>   And past those noisèd Feet
>   A Voice comes yet more fleet –
> "Lo naught contents thee, who content'st not Me."

The fugitive soul can go no further. He has now reached the end
of his tether: all the things in which he had hoped to find rest
have proved unstable. There is no final security in anything
finite – in persons, friends, wealth, possessions, or in attachments of any kind – least of all in the cleverness and deceitful
resources of the ego. How many lives of suffering, disillusionment, bitterness and darkness men may inflict upon themselves
before they come to this point of despair. There is nothing in
which to trust: there is nowhere else to go.

> Naked I wait Thy love's uplifted stroke!
> My harness piece by piece Thou hast hewn from me,
>   And smitten me to my knee;
>   I am defenceless utterly.
>   I slept, methinks, and woke,
> And, slowly gazing, find me stripped in sleep.
> In the rash lustihood of my young powers,
>   I shook the pillaring hours
> And pulled my life upon me; grimed with smears,
> I stand amid the dust o' the mounded years –
> My mangled youth lies dead beneath the heap.
> My days have crackled and gone up in smoke,
> Have puffed and burst as sun-starts on a stream.

"Now it was," said one person,* "that I began to realise how every great sorrow leads us farther and farther out on the promontory of existence. I had come to the uttermost point now – and there was no more.

"I sat alone on the promontory of existence, with the sun and stars gone out, and ice-cold emptiness above me, about me, and in me, on every side.

"But then, my friend, by degrees it dawned on me that there was still something left. There was one little indomitable spark in me, and that began to glow all by itself – as if I were lifted back to the first day of existence, and an eternal will rose up in me, and said: 'Let there be Light.'"

It is at this point of complete darkness, when all else has failed, that many souls have their first glimpse of the Light of God. To awaken the self to make this supreme discovery, the soul may even lead the ego into the darkest depths to make it. There is only God.

*Vide Johan Bojer's novel *The Great Hunger* (Hodder & Stoughton Ltd).

3

The Hound of Heaven (ii)

AT THE POINT OF UTTER DARKNESS AND DESPAIR THE MIND IS SICK.
The person now needs the comfort of human understanding
and the warmth of human love, until the Divine Love, which
alone can cure it, is able to break through.

The mental sickness is shown by the ego's last despairing –
and critical – cry. It blames God – not itself – for the darkness.

> Ah! is Thy love indeed
> A weed, albeit an amaranthine weed,
> Suffering no flowers except its own to mount?
> Ah! must –
> Designer infinite! –
> Ah! must Thou char the wood ere Thou canst limn with it?

Then the ego quickly turns from resentment to self-pity:

> My freshness spent its wavering shower i' the dust;
> And now my heart is as a broken fount,
> Wherein tear-drippings stagnate, spilt down ever
> From the dank thoughts that shiver
> Upon the sighful branches of my mind.
> Such is; what is to be?
> The pulp so bitter, how shall taste and rind?

The soul is now in despair and darkness, and it is at this point
that Francis Thompson makes the first dawn of light appear. He
must have been speaking from experience.

I dimly guess what Time in mists confounds;
Yet ever and anon a trumpet sounds
From the hid battlements of Eternity;
Those shaken mists a space unsettle, then
Round the half-glimpsèd turrets slowly wash again.
    But not ere him who summoneth
    I first have seen, enwound
With glooming robes purpureal, cypress-crowned;
His name I know, and what his trumpet saith.

The first awareness of the fact that there is meaning and significance in his situation has come to him. He know his life's
purpose is somehow linked with the "hid battlements of
Eternity". Even if further mists of suffering close in upon the
view: he has now seen it! He has seen, not a blind impersonal
Fate or Chance sweeping away before it all men's tenderest
hopes and loftiest dreams, but some Loving One whose voice
the winds and waves must obey. He knows what the trumpet
is saying to him. So this life is not all meaningless and dark!
The first rays of the Light of God are dawning. He has learned
enough now to have grounds for trust. He is not yet clear of
the darkness, but he is moving in the right direction. His last
remaining problem is Death, and there still remains with him
a little bitterness as the fugitive says:

    Whether man's heart or life it be which yields
      Thee harvest, must Thy harvest fields
      Be dunged with rotten death?

Can we not all feel deep compassion with this suffering soul?
Have we ever looked on the closed eyes and unresponsive
features of someone who has been dear to us? We have asked
ourselves where the beloved tenant has gone, now that the
empty shell alone remains. Perhaps we have not felt the bitterness of these three lines of Thompson, but we have all felt the
poignancy of Tennyson's lament:

    But Oh for the touch of a vanish'd hand
      And the sound of a voice that is still.

Thompson's great poem of the soul's flight is now reaching

its climax. The Voice to which he has not hitherto listened is now around him "like a bursting Sea". It is saying to him:

"Lo! all things fly thee, for thou fliest Me!"

The divine Voice reminds the fugitive that there is a vital difference between human love and divine Love.

> And human love needs human meriting:
> How has thou merited –
> Of all man's clotted clay the dingiest clot?
> Alack, thou knowest not
> How little worthy of any love thou art!
> Whom wilt thou find to love ignoble thee,
> Save Me, save only Me?
> All which I took from thee I did but take,
> Not for thy harms,
> But just that thou might'st seek it in My arms.
> All which thy child's mistake
> Fancies as lost, I have stored for thee at home:
> Rise, clasp My hand, and come.

What human beings call love is ego-centred. It may have the posture of altruism, but it wants something or someone for itself. What is described as love is often the desire to be loved. It is offered to another person with strings attached. It expects a response, and will fade out if this is not forthcoming. It is an emotion and belongs to the pairs of opposites such as love/hate, etc. True divine Love is not an emotion: it is the natural radiation of the soul, and is a steady flame. It is given freely, expecting nothing in return. It makes no demands. Time does not change it nor does it limit itself. It flows onwards to warm all who are in its path of life. Its prototype is the Father's unchanging love portrayed in the parable of the Prodigal Son.

It is this divine Lover Who has been pursuing the fugitive, and in his foolishness and fear he has been fleeing life after life. The poet has earlier suggested that the fugitive's motivation is essentially ego-centred.

> For though I knew His love, Who followed,
> Yet was I sore adread
> Lest having Him, I might have nought beside.

Here is the great paradox of our being. The Spiritual Path is one in which the divine Lover of man's soul is contending with the selfish lower ruler of our nature – the ego. Once the latter is abandoned or surrendered, – generally a life-long task, the true soul-nature comes into its own. We are then illumined beings, pure channels for divine activity. The paradox is, that in what we imagine is a great renunciation (having nought beside), we become one with the All. Seen from high spiritual levels, there is naught beside the great One-Many. All that we conceive to exist otherwise is in fact illusion, possessing a limited degree of reality only, which we have however to take some account of on our lower levels. The closing lines of the poem present us with sublime Truth, as simple and profound as anything that has come from a poet's pen.

> All which I took from thee I did but take,
> Not for thy harms,
> But just that thou might'st seek it in My arms.
> All which thy child's mistake
> Fancies as lost, I have stored for thee at home:
> Rise, clasp My hand, and come.

They speak of the relationship of all souls to the Father. Though they may sometimes be recalled through tears they bring with them serene depths of Love and Peace from a Master Who offered them to His disciples, saying, "Let not your heart be troubled, neither let it be afraid."

When the path of life seems to lead only through dark valleys, the closing lines are a reminder that as seen from our human standpoint, we are terribly limited and restricted. We do not appreciate properly the greater whole to which our action and life are leading. This consummation is hidden from us until we are illumined.

> Halts by me that footfall:
> Is my gloom, after all,
> Shade of His Hand, outstretched caressingly?
> "Ah, fondest, blindest, weakest,
> I am He Whom thou seekest!
> Thou dravest love from thee, who dravest Me."

How often the things our egos have coveted have proved

their worthlessness! How often what we thought was gloom proved the shade of His Hand outstretched to bless us! As we look back over the years and see the network of paths through which we have moved without any foreknowledge of the places to which we would be led, most of us can say, "I would not have missed that for anything."

"Surely goodness and mercy have followed me all the days of my life, and (someday) I shall dwell in the House of the Lord (i.e., the Kingdom) for ever."

4

Nothing We Love is Lost

THIS IS ONE OF THE GREAT TRUTHS TO BE WRITTEN IN LETTERS OF gold across the pages of life. It is true Love, which, by its very nature confers immortality. This insight should be taken literally, not minimised or ignored as poetic fancy. However imperfectly expressed in words, it expresses on this lower level a principle upon which the Inner Worlds are built. It is our true Love which confers immortality on that which we love; it is His Eternal Love which has conferred immortality on us. The pursuing Lover of man's soul in Francis Thompson's poem reminds us:

> All which thy child's mistake
> Fancies as lost, I have stored for thee at home:
> Rise, clasp My Hand, and come.

This same truth is expressed sensitively and clearly in A.E.'s poem called *Promise*. In his book *Song and its Fountains*, A.E. (George Russell) says some interesting things about how the poem came to him. He says "It was one of the last to come out of the genie in the innermost, and gave promise that whatever wisdom the outer mind had gathered, would not be lost, and that when we went inwards to our own immortal, we should regain all that time had taken away." The poem is of fragile beauty, and has upon it the authentic stamp of the soul's stored inner knowledge.

> Be not so desolate
> Because thy dreams have flown

And the hall of the heart is empty
And silent as stone,
As age left by children
Sad and alone.

Those delicate children,
Thy dreams, still endure:
All pure and lovely things
Wend to the Pure.
Sigh not: unto the fold
Their way was sure.

Thy gentlest dreams, thy frailest,
Even those that were
Born and lost in a heart-beat,
Shall meet thee there.
They are become immortal
In shining air.

The unattainable beauty
The thought of which was pain,
That flickered in eyes and on lips
And vanished again:
That fugitive beauty
Thou shalt attain.

The lights innumerable
That led thee on and on,
The Masque of Time ended,
Shall glow into one,
It shall be with thee for ever
Thy travel done.

Here in a physical body, we are only able to look out through five narrow slits – the senses. We are also limited by that little moving aperture which we call the *present* moment from vistas of the past and future. We are living as prisoners of Time, Space, and Appearance. How restricted is our knowledge and how little we can see of the Pattern of Life! We come into the home of particular parents at a particular point of history. The friends whom we meet, the rivals with whom we contend, the opportunities and frustrations that occur, the work which we seek to accomplish, the health which aids or hinders us, and the environment which we share with others, seem to be given to us without rhyme or reason. Sooner or later we have to face inescapable questions. Has life meaning and does chance or accident enter into it? Is there Love at the heart of this mystery? If only we could be lifted above the confusing spectacle of the moment, and see that life is wholly meaningful and all undergirded by Love!

What he called "the genie in the innermost" gave A.E. this assurance which he expressed in his poem *Promise*. My own genie re-echoes the same truth. Nothing and no-one whom we truly love is ever lost, but until we completely understand the nature of Time we shall remain with veiled sight. In some high mystical states the unreality of Time seems evident, but as soon as we are back in the region of mind, both time and change thrust themselves upon us. "The Masque of Time" makes possible human life as we know it, but the real life is lived when the masque is over.

A.E.'s poem, assured, delicate and beautiful, has all the marks of inspiration and authentic knowledge. Nothing is too good to be true. If God is Infinite Love, our highest dreams must fall short of the Reality which He conserves. Even our noblest and most wonderful imaginings are a thousand times too poor to express the Truth.

The eternity of that which we truly love is also a notable element in Robert Browning's faith and outlook. The following lines taken from his poem *Abt Vogler* are among the finest he ever wrote:

> Therefore to whom turn I but to Thee, the ineffable
>   Name?
>   Builder and maker, Thou, of houses not made with
>   hands!
> What, have fear of change from Thee who are ever the
>   same?
>   Doubt that Thy power can fill the heart that Thy
>   power expands?
> There shall never be one lost good! What was, shall live
>   as before;
>   The evil is null, is nought, is silence implying sound;
> What was good, shall be good, with for evil, so much
>   good more;

On the earth the broken arcs; in the heaven a perfect
  round.

All we have willed or hoped or dreamed of good, shall
  exist:
    Not its semblance, but itself; no beauty, nor good,
      nor power
Whose voice has gone forth, but each survives for the
  melodist
    When eternity affirms the conception of an hour.
The high that proved too high, the heroic for earth too
  hard,
    The passion that left the ground to lose itself in the
      sky,
    Are music sent up to God by the lover and the bard;
      Enough that He heard it once: we shall hear it by
        and by.

How few of the dreams of men are realised! A man may give
his devotion and service to a cause which others destroy soon
after he has gone. Looked at from the human level, and as-
sessed as earthly judgments go, a man's life may appear to be a
failure. A.E. and Robert Browning, in their poems, are inviting
us to take a deeper view. The physical level which to the eye
of sense seems so important, is regarded by them as quite
secondary. The will which aimed at noble ends, the dreams
which were unfulfilled, "the high that proved too high" – all
these are treasured by Him Who inspired them. The beauty
which the artist tried to capture, but which eluded him; the
music which haunted the musician, but could not be expressed;
the love which flowed between two souls whom fate parted; the
child whose life closed before it had scarcely begun; the un-
finished symphonies of human life are not lost, or blown away
by the winds of Time. They are precious to the Father in Whose
keeping they remain, and they will be given back in their perfection at the close of the journey.

  On one occasion when he was visiting London, Rabindranath Tagore told his friend C. F. Andrews of three great
waves of sorrow which had rolled over him. First he lost his
wife. A little later he lost his daughter, and finally cholera took
away his only son. He told Andrews that in the end, "he came

to look upon Death as no longer the King of Terrors, but altogether as a cherished friend". He said to Andrews, "You know, I came to feel that even if an atom in the universe seemed lost, it never really could be lost. I knew at last what death was – it was perfection."

It may be appropriate to close this meditation with a poem written by a courageous woman. It was found among Emily Brontë's papers after her death at the age of thirty-nine. In her lonely life at the Haworth parsonage on the Yorkshire moors, she discovered the same certainty.

> No coward soul is mine,
> No trembler in the world's storm-troubled sphere:
>   I see Heaven's glories shine,
> And faith shines equal, arming me from fear.
>
> O God within my breast,
> Almighty, ever-present Deity!
>   Life – that in me has rest
> As I – undying Life – have power in Thee!
>
>   . . .
>
> With wide-embracing love
> Thy Spirit animates eternal years,
>   Pervades and broods above,
> Changes, sustains, dissolves, creates, and rears.
>
> Though earth and man were gone,
> And suns and universes ceased to be,
>   And Thou wert left alone,
> Every existence would exist in Thee.
>
> There is no room for Death,
> Nor atom that his might could render void:
>   Thou – Thou art Being and Breath,
> And what Thou are may never be destroyed.

5

The Immanent and the Omnipresent

I THINK WE SHOULD RIGHTLY PAY ATTENTION TO WHAT MAY BE called a spiritual Last Will & Testament. A person may leave behind for posterity a few heart-felt words as though to say, "This is what life has taught me. Forget everything else, if you will, but this I offer to you for your remembrance." The last lines of Emily Brontë have just been quoted – the lines of a courageous woman who approached at times close to the Mysteries, and knew her soul's immortality. The six verses which follow were found among Francis Thompson's papers after his death. They are usually entitled *The Kingdom of God*. In a footnote to the *Collected Poems* there is the comment:

". . . The prevision of Heaven in Earth and God in man, pervading his earlier published verse, is here accented by poignantly local and personal allusion. For in these triumphing stanzas he held in retrospect those days and nights of human dereliction he spent beside London's river, and in the shadow – but all radiance to him – of Charing Cross."

> O world invisible, we view thee,
> O world intangible, we touch thee,
> O world unknowable, we know thee,
> Inapprehensible, we clutch thee!
>
> Does the fish soar to find the ocean,
> The eagle plunge to find the air –
> That we ask of the stars in motion
> If they have rumour of thee there?
>
> Not where the wheeling systems darken,

And our benumbed conceiving soars! –
The drift of pinions, would we hearken,
Beats at our own clay-shuttered doors.

The angels keep their ancient places; –
Turn but a stone, and start a wing!
  'Tis ye, 'tis your estrangèd faces,
That miss the many-splendoured thing.

But (when so sad thou canst not sadder)
Cry; – and upon thy so sore loss
Shall shine the traffic of Jacob's ladder
Pitched betwixt Heaven and Charing Cross.

Yea, in the night, my Soul, my daughter,
Cry, – clinging Heaven by the hems;
And lo, Christ walking on the water
Not of Gennesareth, but Thames.

All down the ages men have described themselves as searching for God. Some have gone into the deserts, some have lived in forest retreats or in remote mountain caves. Some have shunned human society, living in frugality and asceticism, to eliminate that which they believed was a barrier to spiritual awareness. They have entered monasteries, they have scourged themselves, they have fasted and deprived themselves of sleep, they have arranged to be walled-up in stone huts in the darkness, and they have fatigued their minds by strange practices. However mistaken some of the methods have been, their existence reminds us of the intensity of the longing in man's soul for immediate knowledge of his true nature and direct contact with the Source of his being. The poet has suggested that God is not hiding from us although we may be insensitive to His presence. He writes of "our clay-shuttered doors", a reference no doubt to the restrictions placed upon us by the physical body. He speaks also of "our estrangèd faces", which suggests that we are not looking in the right direction. He does tell us, out of his own sad life-experience, that when the soul is desperate, – "so sad thou can'st not sadder", the cry is answered from above. The soul is shown the Spiritual Path, by climbing which she will in the end reach the Kingdom of God.

The nineteenth-century hymn-writer Frederick Faber expressed a sense of God Immanent in many verses. Here are three of them which express this idea simply:

> Twice have I erred: a distant God
>   Was what I could not bear;
> Sorrow and cares were at my side;
>   I longed to have Him there.

> But God is never so far off
>   As even to be near;
> He is within: our spirit is
>   The home He holds most dear.

> So all the while I thought myself
>   Homeless, forlorn and weary,
> Missing my joy, I walked the earth
>   Myself God's sanctuary.

This view would be supported by the great insight of Vedanta, "That art Thou". But between knowing this with the mind as a philosophical truth and knowing it mystically as an immediate experience, there is the long arduous journey of the Spiritual Path. This is a life-long task, and may be indeed a task of many lives. To know Him truly is the greatest and most sublime attainment of mortal man. This is the Pearl of Great Price and qualifies the soul to become a Being of Light, an Immortal.

In his poem *Saul*, Browning attempts to express the witness of Nature, and of all created things to this Immanent Divinity.

> I spoke as I saw:
> I report as a man may of God's work – all's love yet all's law.
> Now I lay down the judgeship He lent me. Each faculty
>   tasked
> To perceive Him, has gained an abyss, where a dew drop
>   was asked.
> Have I knowledge? confounded it shrivels at Wisdom laid
>   bare.
> Have I forethought? how purblind, how blank, to the
>   Infinite Care!
> Do I task any faculty highest, to image success?
> I but open my eyes, – and perfection no more and no less,

In the kind I imagined, full fronts me, and God is seen God
In the star, in the stone, in the flesh, in the soul and the clod.
And thus looking within and around me, I ever renew
(With that stoop of the soul which in bending upraises it too)
The submission of man's nothing-perfect to God's all-
    complete,
As by each new obeisance in spirit, I climb to His feet.

It is a universe full of wonder where thousands of patterns
inter-weave and are inter-related. Each field of scientific en-
quiry has its roots in some mystery, such as the nature of life or
of energy, of space and of time. Behind all this observed world
is the almost unknown world of Mind. Sustaining this vast
imponderable world of cosmic mind is the fact of Consciousness, Spirit, Reality, or God. (The term we prefer does not
matter.) The mystics are persons like ourselves, but they have
effectively undertaken the disciplines of the Spiritual Path.
They have longed to know Reality, and through their aspirations, longings and hard work they have been granted some
awareness of that which they sought.

Great souls visit our planet from time to time. They come to
help onward those who are ready to make the effort. The greatest ones are described as Enlightened, for they are fully conscious on all levels of their unity with God. It is through their
lives and their testimony that we know that God, the Supreme
Reality is Infinite Love, Bliss, and Consciousness, and that every
soul is a part of that Reality (though it may not yet be conscious
of it). To quote Faber once more:

> Thus doth Thy hospitable greatness lie
>   Outside us like a boundless sea;
> We cannot lose ourselves where all is home,
>   Nor drift away from Thee.

Three or four thousand years ago, Moses said to the people
of Israel – and it is still true:
"The Eternal God is thy refuge, and underneath are the
Everlasting Arms."

6

That Immortal Sea

WORDSWORTH'S GREAT *Ode on Intimations of Immortality from Recollections of Early Childhood* is for me one of the glories of the English tongue. Its spiritual insights give it greatness on a high level, and the poet was inspired by noble language to convey them. The theme that he develops is this.

In the years of childhood he had felt a very deep kinship with Nature, which seemed to him "apparell'd in celestial light". With the passing years, something has changed within him, and he asks:

> Whither is fled the visionary gleam?
> Where is it now, the glory and the dream?

Reflecting upon this, he recognises that the soul has pre-existed this life, and that when it reincarnates it comes here "trailing clouds of glory". As the years pass, this light fades, and veils of illusion slowly wrap it around so that it begins to

> forget the glories he hath known,
> And that imperial palace whence he came.

On looking still further, the poet sees that nothing he has loved has been lost. It is all stored in the soul's treasury of Beauty and Wisdom.

> Yet in my heart of hearts I feel your might;
> I only have relinquished one delight
> To live beneath your more habitual sway.

At this deep level of his being Wordsworth says,

> To me the meanest flower that blows can give
> Thoughts that do often lie too deep for tears.

Wordsworth will always have a special place among the Nature-mystics, able to express the emotions which others feel, but cannot capture in language. The music of the Great Mother speaks clearly to him, and his genius helps us to hear it too. In these days of conducted tours with an eye on the clock, few could say:

> I wander'd lonely as a cloud
> That floats on high o'er vales and hills

but Wordsworth offers us the magic carpet of his words so that in some realm of faery within the mind the golden daffodils by Ullswater are always growing.

> There was a time when meadow, grove, and stream,
> The earth, and every common sight
> > To me did seem
> > Apparell'd in celestial light,
> The glory and the freshness of a dream.
> It is not now as it hath been of yore;
> > Turn wheresoe'er I may,
> > By night or day,
> The things which I have seen I now can see no more.
> > The rainbow comes and goes,
> > And lovely is the rose;
> > The moon doth with delight
> Look round her when the heavens are bare;
> > Waters on a starry night
> > Are beautiful and fair;
> > The sunshine is a glorious birth;
> > But yet I know, where'er I go,
> That there hath passed away a glory from the earth.

The poet looks within, and realises that the change is within himself, not in the world outside. He jolts himself out of this mood of sadness, for his deeper being is fully aware that the mood is at variance with the happiness and peace around him.

> The fullness of your bliss, I feel – I feel it all,
>> O evil day! if I were sullen
>> While Earth herself is adorning
>> This sweet May morning;

Yet in honesty to himself he has to face the fact that all things are witnesses to change:

>> The pansy at my feet
>> Doth the same tale repeat:
> Whither is fled the visionary gleam?
> Where is it now, the glory and the dream?

His higher Self then brings forth the insights:

> Our birth is but a sleep and a forgetting;
> The South that rises with us, our life's Star,
>> Hath had elsewhere its setting
>> And cometh from afar;
>> Not in entire forgetfulness,
>> And not in utter nakedness,
> But trailing clouds of glory do we come
>> From God Who is our home:
> Heaven lies about us in our infancy!
> Shades of the prison-house begin to close
>> Upon the growing Boy,
> But he beholds the light, and whence it flows,
>> He sees it in his joy;
>> The Youth, who daily farther from the east
>> Must travel, still is Nature's priest,
>> And by the vision splendid
>> Is on his way attended;
> At length the man perceives it die away,
> And fade into the light of common day.

> Earth fills her lap with pleasures of her own;
> Yearnings she hath in her own natural kind,
> And, even with something of a mother's mind

And no unworthy aim,
The homely nurse doth all she can
To make her foster-child, her inmate, Man,
Forget the glories he hath known,
And that imperial palace whence he came.

Then he addresses the child (which we may imagine sleeping peacefully in its cot). Has a baby every been addressed with such solemnity before?

Thou whose exterior semblance doth belie
Thy soul's immensity;
Thou best philosopher, who yet dost keep
Thy heritage, thou eye among the blind,
That, deaf and silent, read'st the eternal deep,
Haunted for ever by the eternal Mind,
Mighty prophet! Seer blest!
On whom those truths do rest
Which we are toiling all our lives to find,
In darkness lost, the darkness of the grave;
Thou, over whom thy Immortality
Broods like the day, a master o'er a slave,
A Presence which is not to be put by;
Thou little child, yet glorious in the might
Of heaven-born freedom on thy being's height,
Why with such earnest pains dost thou provoke
The years to bring the inevitable yoke,
Thus blindly with thy blessedness at strife?

These thoughts lead the poet into a mood of quiet joy and gratitude, where he gives thanks and praise for life's best and greatest gifts to him. The soul of Wordsworth is now speaking and it touches a mountain peak of inspiration.

The thought of our past years in me doth breed
Perpetual benediction: not indeed
For that which is most worthy to be blest,
Delight and liberty, the simple creed
Of Childhood, whether busy or at rest,
With new-fledged hope still fluttering in his breast:

> Not for these I raise
> The song of thanks and praise;
> But for those obstinate questionings
> Of sense and outward things,
> Fallings from us, vanishings,
> Blank misgivings of a creature
> Moving about in worlds not realised,
> High instincts, before which our mortal nature
> Did tremble like a guilty thing surprised:

The "high instincts" are the soul's insights into many world-levels of consciousness to which we belong – and before this vision our mere physical nature stands abashed and humbled. His gratitude is particularly felt:

> . . . for those first affections,
> Those shadowy recollections,
> Which, be they what they may,
> Are yet the fountain-light of all our day,
> Are yet a master-light of all our seeing;
> Uphold us – cherish – and have power to make
> Our noisy years seem moments in the being
> Of the eternal Silence: truths that wake,
> To perish never;
> Which neither listlessness, nor mad endeavour
> Nor man nor boy
> Nor all that is at enmity with joy,
> Can utterly abolish or destroy!
> Hence, in a season of calm weather
> Though inland far we be,
> Our souls have sight of that immortal sea
> Which brought us hither;
> Can in a moment travel thither –
> And see the children sport upon the shore,
> And hear the mighty waters rolling evermore.

Wordsworth realises that although the past radiance has gone, the essential Joy remains imperishable in his heart and soul. His Ode concludes on a note of greater sensitivity and compassion for the world around him.

What though the radiance which was once so bright
Be now for ever taken from my sight,
    Though nothing can bring back the hour
Of splendour in the grass, of glory in the flower;
      We will grieve not, rather find
      Strength in what remains behind;
      In the primal sympathy
      Which having been must ever be;
      In the soothing thoughts that spring
      Out of human suffering;
      In the faith that looks through death,
In years that bring the philosophic mind.

And O, ye Fountains, Meadows, Hills, and Groves,
Forbode not any severing of our loves!
Yet in your heart of hearts I feel your might;
I only have relinquished one delight
To live beneath your more habitual sway;
I love the brooks which down their channels fret
Even more than when I tripp'd lightly as they;
The innocent brightness of a new-born day
      Is lovely yet;
The clouds that gather round the setting sun
Do take a sober colouring from an eye
That hath kept watch o'er man's mortality;
Another race hath been, and other palms are won.
Thanks to the human heart by which we live,
Thanks to its tenderness, its joys, and fears,
To me the meanest flower that blows can give
Thoughts that do often lie too deep for tears.

I felt like that on one occasion in winter when I had just put a log on the fire. A compassionate friend who was there, knelt by the hearthside in great concern, using bare hands and a sheet of paper to try to save a few insects which had come out of the log and were seeking an escape from the heat and flames.

Is there a meaning in life – in *all* life – beyond these outer appearances? If we could bring to our seeing, enough sensitivity, love and understanding, we should find the Divine Presence everywhere. What God loves cannot be lost, and what *we* truly love cannot be lost. A.E. expressed it thus, "When we go in to our own immortal Self, we shall find there all that we imagined Time had taken away."

Perhaps the very mystery of Time will drive us at last to an awareness of the Changeless, whose first and last and most wonderful Name is Love.

7

Smile at Time *

IS IT A FOOLISH OR MEANINGLESS QUESTION TO ASK "WHY DOES Time exist?" We are all immersed in it, and cannot by an effort of the mind imagine our selves out of its relentless grasp. Mystical experiences however, offer us some interesting clues. Related below is the experience of a lady who had been under an anaesthetic. She knew that she had experienced something quite significant, and for two or three days tried unsuccessfully to recall it. The memory of it started to return about eight or nine weeks after the operation, although the complete recovery of it "with clarity and certainty" was spread over two or three weeks. Struggling with words she wrote,

All things seemed to be understandable to me. I had a certain, clear, knowledge of life. I could see and understand all activities on all levels. What was going on in the operating theatre was only part of it. There was also the cycle of birth, life and death, and all the endeavours, struggle and mystery connected with this cycle. Something inside (or outside) me, said, "*It has always been the same*". We do this, we do that, we anguish, we struggle, we love, we try to be happy, but the cycle never really changes. I was vividly aware of another reality outside this cycle, and momentarily I was equally at home in both states – the life cycle, and the other reality which was both part of it and outside it.

When I first began to recall this experience I was very

---

* This happy phrase I owe to Constance Sitwell's book of that title.

depressed. It seemed to me it indicated that life and all its endeavours was a gigantic terrible hoax which human beings had perpetuated as some sort of antidote to their dreadful isolation. "If this is all," I thought, "then everything is a hollow mockery. It is all meaningless illusion." However, in another few days I felt reassured. I realised that I fully and peacefully accepted the truth, "*It has always been the same*", but what I now felt was an acutely heightened awareness of everything around me, which had a quality or character I had never seen or sensed before. I was more aware of the inter-relations of things, nature, and people, and had some understanding of myself as being part of the universal whole.

In this remarkable experience her consciousness moved from the ego-level which was concerned with the life-cycle in which "*It has always been the same*" up to the soul-level, the other reality "which was both part of it and outside it".

Rupert Brooke's poem which he calls *Dining Room Tea* des-cribes a mystical experience in which the sense of time-succession is suspended. It is a well-known characteristic of high levels of consciousness.

The poet has described a familiar and happy scene of laughter amid the fellowship of a little group of friends. Then comes the mystical element:

> Till suddenly, and otherwhence,
> I looked upon your innocence.
> For lifted clear and still and strange
> From the dark woven flow of change
> Under a vast and starless sky
> I saw the immortal moment lie.
> One instant I, an instant, knew
> As God knows all. And it and you
> I, above Time, oh, blind! could see
> In witless immortality.
> I saw the marble cup; the tea,
> Hung on the air, an amber stream;
> I saw the fire's unglittering gleam,
> The painted flame, the frozen smoke.
> No more the flooding lamplight broke
> On flying eyes and lips and hair;

But lay, but slept unbroken there,
On stiller flesh, and body breathless,
And lips and laughter stayed and deathless,
And words on which no silence grew,
Light was more alive than you.

Till suddenly, and otherwhence,
I looked on your magnificence.
I saw the stillness and the light,
And you, august, immortal, white,
Holy and strange; and every glint
Posture and jest and thought and tint
Freed from the mask of transiency,
Triumphant in eternity,
Immote, immortal.

        Dazed at length
Human eyes grew, mortal strength
Wearied; and Time began to creep.
Change closed about me like a sleep.
Light glinted on the eyes I loved.
The cup was filled. The bodies moved.
The drifting petal came to ground.
The laughter chimed its perfect round.
The broken syllable was ended.
And I, so certain and so friended,
How could I cloud, or how distress,
The heaven of your unconsciousness?
Or shake at Time's sufficient spell,
Stammering of lights unutterable?
The eternal holiness of you,
The timeless end, you never knew,
The peace that lay, the light that shone.
You never knew that I had gone
A million miles away, and stayed
A million years . . .

The sense of change, and therefore of movement through time, is linked up with our restriction to the "specious present". As we are able to rise in consciousness to higher levels which have a wider "specious present" this sense of change gets less. We increasingly see things as they *are*, not as they are becoming.

On a high level, temporarily transcending mind, the poet has
been aware of the true Self or Soul of the person with whom he
was concerned. He speaks of "lights unutterable", the "eternal
holiness of you", and of the "peace that lay, the light that
shone". On such high levels we are aware that Love is the
foundation-principle of existence, that it is of the essential
nature of Being, and that it does not depend upon, although it
creates the forms through which it is expressed.

Even on the familiar physical level we constantly recognise
an element which time cannot destroy. In the relationship of
mother and child, while there is usually much of the instinctive
drive, we can generally see something persistent and precious,
rooted at a higher level. The outer form is constantly changing:
the baby becomes a child, the child becomes a boy or girl—then
follows adolescence and maturity. In spite of the changing
forms a true Love may be enduring unchanged.

Constantly seeking for the Essence within the Soul of man,
James Cousins wrote of it:

> There, in a garden paradised,
> I keep the Soul's eternal tryst.
> She hangs her silence as a screen.
> She waits me, felt, but ah! unseen.
>
> She will not mix with mine her name
> Till I can burn as crystal flame;
> With God and Life and Her made one,
> Espoused of all, and bound to none:
>
> Life's loves with little passions play
> In satisfactions of a day.
> Love that from life's dim first doth wend
> Finds its fulfilment in the end.
>
> . . .
>
> To no less heavenly conquest, She
> Yieldeth her white virginity.
> Yea, though I woo in countless ways,
> Still She eludes my longing gaze.
>
> Only God's eye in secret sees
> Her veiled celestial sanctities,
> Till I, grown Godlike, claim my prize –
> And perish in Her burning eyes!

Love and Death are commonly pictured as old antagonists, but such a view is superficial. The wheel of lives and deaths turns, and inevitably brings souls together again in different relationships until at last they break free from the wheel into that true freedom where Eternal true Being remains. Hugh I'A. Fausset has well said, "Love runs into the arms of death to find, not destruction, but the beauty and mercy of life."

The poignancy of human separation by physical death has inevitably led to much moving poetry, but what is expressed by the poet may often fall far short of the truth. Unless he is a mystic of a high order he will have the same limitations as ordinary men. Illumined souls, conscious on many levels, do not react to grief as we ordinary people do – not because they are insensitive – but because they have been "freed from the mask of transiency". We too can learn to smile at Time when we have once seen how superficial our judgment is because of our restriction to the "specious present" moment. Yet our hearts tell us with certainty that what we have loved and known, while expressed to us through sense-data, has its roots in higher levels and higher worlds. Several of the finest English poets say to us "Learn to accept transiency and let it make you more appreciative of what you have. Live fully in the present and thus you will leave behind no room for regret." The advice is good, but the viewpoint is too limited. If, like the mystics, they could have been lifted for a moment to see beyond the veil of appearance, they would have been aware of the everlasting Glory, Joy and Love around them all the time, from which there is no real separation.

When I reflect upon the many millions of lives cut short in the holocausts of this century, and of the countless millions of those who loved them and felt grief, sorrow, and suffering at their passing, it is good to remember that some of the soldier-poets knew and tried to express the truth. Before he passed over in 1915 Rupert Brooke could write:

We have found safety with all things undying,
    The winds, and morning, tears of men, and mirth,
    The deep might, and birds singing, and clouds flying,
    And sleep, and freedom, and the autumnal earth.
We have built a house that is not for Time's throwing.

We have gained a peace unshaken by pain for ever.
War knows no power. Safe shall be my going,
    Secretly armed against all death's endeavour;
Safe though all safety's lost; safe where men fall;
    And if these poor limbs die – safest of all.

I share the certainty that we are building a house that is "not for Time's throwing". Therefore we can smile at Time.

8

Divine Love

THE SEVENTEENTH-CENTURY ENGLISH CLERGYMAN GEORGE Herbert wrote a quantity of religious verse which found a place in an early volume of the Oxford Series of Poets. Although the religious idiom of his time gives much of it an archaic flavour to modern readers, some of his poems combine great insight with an expression of devotion which is timeless. Here is one which is outstanding:

Love bade me welcome; yet my soul drew back,
      Guilty of dust and sin.
But quick-eyed Love, observing me grow slack
      From my first entrance in,
Drew nearer to me, sweetly questioning
      If I lack'd anything.

"A guest," I answer'd, "worthy to be here":
      Love said, "You shall be he."
"I, the unkind, ungrateful? Ah my dear,
      I cannot look on Thee."
Love took my hand, and smiling did reply,
      "Who made the eyes but I?"

"Truth, Lord; but I have marr'd them; let my shame
      Go where it doth deserve."
"And know you not," says Love, "Who bore the blame?"
      "My dear, then I will serve."
"You must sit down," says Love, "and taste my meat."
      So I did sit and eat.

I think of it as portraying what may well have been the state of mind of the Prodigal Son as he sat down to the feast of welcome which the Father provided to celebrate his return. Everyone who has studied this greatest of the parables of Jesus recognises that it is a profound allegory of the journey of the soul of man. In Herbert's poem Divine Love is personified as the Host, uniting strength, compassion and infinite tenderness.

In the following poem called *The Penalty of Love* by S. R. Lysaght, Love is personified as the guest:

> If Love should count you worthy, and should deign
>   One day to seek your door and be your guest,
>   Pause! ere you draw the bolt and bid him rest,
> If in your old content you would remain.
> For not alone he enters: in his train
>   Are angels of the mist, the lonely quest,
>   Dreams of the unfulfilled and unpossessed,
> And sorrow, and Life's immemorial pain.
> He wakes desires you never may forget,
>   He shows you stars you never saw before,
>   He makes you share with him, for evermore,
> The burden of the world's divine regret.
> How wise you were to open not! – and yet,
>   How poor if you should turn him from the door.

Divine Love stands knocking at the door of the human heart, and when He enters as a guest, He becomes the host. Two disciples on the road to Emmaus made that discovery. Jesus overtook them as a stranger. They invited Him into their house to share a meal with them, but it was He who broke the bread and blessed their home. When they recognised Him he vanished out of their sight. In doing this He was reminding them that they must look within, not without, for the abiding Presence. It is safe to say that this climactic experience would be the most treasured memory of their life: it would be told to their children and their children's children.

In Lysaght's poem Love is described as driving out the old complacency, speaking of the necessity of becoming one with the joys, sufferings, and needs of all others, human and non-human, tied up with us in the bundle of life. Every sufferer is a brother or sister for whom we are willing to do as much as for any relative or friend. Our old content based upon self-centred-ness falls away. We become sensitive to "sorrow and life's immemorial pain". Wordsworth called it "the still, sad, music of humanity". This increasing and ever-widening senstivity brings ample compensations as we see "stars we never saw before". In such unbarring of the door to Love there is enor-mous vulnerability, but the answer to all those who decry it or hesitate was made by Jesus when He said, "Except a grain of wheat fall into the ground and die it abideth alone, but if it die, it beareth much fruit."

For some, the Spiritual Path may begin from a point of des-pair and disillusionment with ordinary life; for others, from an experience of great suffering or loss, and in others, from an intense desire and questing to know the meaning of life. Such questing must be sustained by both the mind and heart. "Lovest thou Me?" is the eternally relevant question for every seeker. Later, there will follow the more searching question, "Lovest thou Me more than these?" *These* may be wife, husband, children, lover, possessions, and even life itself. If the intellectual objects: "How can I love someone Whom I don't know?" Pascal answered him when he said, "Human things have to be known to be loved; Divine things have to be loved to be known."

Doubtless here there is something of a paradox. As mortals it appears that we can only love that which is in some sense personalised and finite: we do not know how to love a Principle or a Power or even the Creator of the Universe. The testing of our love for God must therefore lie in how much we love *all* others. Jesus recognised this when He said, "Inasmuch as ye did it unto one of these, My brethren, even these least, ye did it unto Me."

The sage Mirdad* has truly said, "You live that you may learn to love. You love that you may learn to live. No other lesson is required of Man."

> Belovèd, let us love.
> Love is of God;

---

* Mikhail Naimy *The Book of Mirdad*, Chapter II of this book is worthy to rank with St Paul's great hymn to Love (I Cor. XIII).

In God alone hath Love
  Its true abode

Belovèd, let us love:
  In Love is Light,
And he who loveth not,
  Dwelleth in night.

Belovèd, let us love
  For only thus
Shall we behold that God
  Who loveth us.

9

Human Love

IT IS UNFORTUNATE THAT IN THE ENGLISH LANGUAGE WE USE
the one word *love* to stand for several elements of a different
order. The highest Love of which we can conceive is divine in its
nature. Its origin is in God and therefore it is a natural radiation of the soul of man, when that soul begins to unfold. It has
been counted by the philosophers as one of the supreme values
along with Truth, Beauty and Wisdom: these are the founda-
tion principles of existence. In the highest human love some of
this soul-element doubtless plays an important part. We recognise it by certain marks: a complete self-giving with no expectation of return, no conditions attached, no possessiveness
involved, no variability or fluctuation. This is rare however,
and most human love depends on mutuality, expects some
response, is possessive and attached, thus reducing the freedom
of the one beloved. On the highest human level, a person may
be willing to give everything away, even life itself, to serve what
is believed to be the best interests of the beloved. Certainly we
are dealing with a most powerful force in human life. In the
greater part of human love we may recognise karmic links between individuals arising from many different relationships in
past lives, and these may bring emotional turmoil into the present. It has to be freely admitted that in our modern civilisation
much of the so-called "love" is little more than a manifestation
of powerful instinctive drives operating not far below the level
of conscious behaviour. The term "love" is quite inappro-
priate, and should be replaced by "desire". The sage Mirdad
speaks of the love of man for woman and *vice versa* as only "a
very distant token" of true Love; even the love of parents for

their children, he assigns to "the threshold of Love's temple". One cannot doubt that he is right in this assessment. Most human relationships described as "loving" embody elements from very different levels of the human self – and in very varying proportions.

As we might expect, love between man and woman – romantic love, as it is described – has certainly given rise to some exquisite poetry in the English tongue. This could be anticipated, for the range and delicacy of the emotions involved is often one which prose is too clumsy to express. Moreover to the delicacy of the emotions is sometimes added the most sensitive aspirations of the heart and soul. Here is a poem of James H. Cousins which illustrates both a realisation of the eternity of true love, and the infinite possibilities of its growth.

> Since first my heart awoke to winds that blew
> Infinite need, lo! it has climbed its stair
> Of dreams, and to the unresponsive air
> Stretched hungry hands, and called and called for you.
>
> Then, answerless, it moulded of the dew
> And splendid noons and sunset's tumbled hair
> And deep sea-music, something more than fair
> Which long it strove to know, yet never knew.
>
> But now your cheek is warm against my cheek,
> And is love satisfied? Nay! evermore
> Your hands are full of promise, and your eyes
> Gleam with a spirit-light I still must seek
> But never find; for joy has joy in store
> And heaven another heaven within its skies.

Of true Love – a component in the highest human love – Tagore has some great insights to offer us:

"Real Love is always a wonder. We can never take it for granted . . . It gives one a hope that truth is more than appearance, and that we deserve more than we can claim with apparent reason. Love is for the unlimited in us, not for the one who is so loudly evident . . . We could never be certain that we are more in truth than we are in fact, if we were not loved."

Cousins, in another poem expresses a similar thought:

Oh! we who have in will essayed
To love in the celestial way,
Dare not our mutual gods degrade
Through frail alliances with clay.

Not the most poignant inward reach
Of trellised fingers, mingled eyes,
Nor all the songs in love's warm speech
That holy passion pacifies.

Higher than exile's aching walls,
Clearer than joy in union lit,
Through life's frail finitudes it calls
From infinite to infinite.

And not alone doth love invite
Our hearts in that high quest to go;
All life's desirings of delight
Press on with us; for well we know

What comrades crowd the spiral track
Trod out in star-dust and in loam,
Where pressing on is hastening back,
And even truant feet go home;

For mixed in seraph, sage and elf
In wandering waters, captive trees,
Life through enlargements of itself
Moves on to mightier syntheses.

Cousins' reference to "exile's aching walls" is a reminder that perhaps the most poignantly beautiful English poetry has grown out of a relationship felt between two persons who have been parted by the nature of the pattern of life. While true Love (being of soul for soul) is beyond the corroding processes of time, there must remain for mortals some grief at those barriers which separate them from companionship. If they are spiritually advanced souls they will not allow this grief to obsess them or retard their homeward footsteps. Such a spiritual achievement may be the hardest of tests, but may bring the greatest of rewards. Several of the poems of Alice Meynell have expressed the poignancy of this human situation perfectly. Here are two of them. The first is called *To the Beloved*.

Ah, not more subtly silence strays
    Amongst the winds, between the voices,
Mingling alike with pensive lays,
    And with the music that rejoices,
Than thou art present in my days.

My silence, life returns to thee
    In all the pauses of her breath,
Hush back to rest the melody
    That out of thee awakeneth;
And thou, wake ever, wake for me!

Thou art like silence all unvexed,
    Though wild words part my soul from thee.
Thou art like silence unperplexed,
    A secret and a mystery
Between one footfall and the next.

Most dear pause in a mellow lay!
    Thou art inwoven with every air.
With thee the wildest tempests play,
    And snatches of thee everywhere
Make little heavens throughout a day.

Darkness and solitude shine for me.
    For life's fair outward part are rife
The silver noises; let them be.
    It is the very soul of life
Listens for thee, listens for thee.

O pause between the sobs of cares;
    O thought within all thought that is;
Trance between laughters unawares:
    Thou art the shape of melodies,
And thou the ecstasy of prayers.

Equally beautiful is Alice Meynell's poem called *Regrets*.

As when the seaward ebbing tide doth pour
    Out by the low sand spaces,
The parting waves slip back to clasp the shore
    With lingering embraces,

So in the tide of life that carries me

From where thy true heart dwells,
Waves of my thought and memories turn to thee
With lessening farewells;

Waving of hands; dreams, when the day forgets;
A care half lost in cares;
The saddest of my verses; dim regrets;
Thy name among my prayers.

I would the day might come, so waited for,
So patiently besought,
When I, returning, should fill up once more
Thy desolated thought;

And fill thy loneliness that lies apart
In still persistent pain.
Shall I content thee, O thou broken heart,
As the tide comes again,

And brims the little sea-shore lakes, and sets
Seaweeds afloat, and fills
The silent pools, rivers and rivulets
Among the inland hills?

George Russell once wrote that he had endeavoured to make all his poetry transparencies into the Spirit. Perhaps one of the best measures of greatness in poetry is its ability to do this for us. The magic of human love is often able to lift ordinary mortals a little nearer to the Spirit, and for its power to do this let us give thanks. All Nature is endowed with the power to evoke this emotion. Thus Henry van Dyke wrote a pleasant lyric called *Love's Nearness*, the translation of a poem of Goethe:

I think of thee, when golden sunbeams shimmer
Across the sea;
And when the waves reflect the moon's pale glimmer
I think of thee.

I see thy form, when down the distant highway
The dust-clouds rise;
In deepest night, above the mountain by-way
I see thine eyes.

I hear thee when the ocean-tides returning

Loudly rejoice;
And on the lonely moor, in stillness yearning
I hear thy voice.

I dwell with thee: though thou art far removèd,
Yet art thou near.
The sun goes down, the stars shine out, – Belovèd
Ah, wert thou here!

The constant orientation of human love towards the beloved
is perhaps an early step which anticipates those high states of
the soul, in which, the mystics tell us they see God everywhere.
The Divine Love has no boundaries or limitations, and Browning spoke of this:

. . . perfection no more and no less,
In the kind I imagined full-fronts me, and God is
seen God
In the star, in the stone, in the flesh, in the soul, and
the clod.

George Russell once wrote, "What the lover discovers in the
beloved is the beauty of poetry which is in his own being. But
it may take hundreds of thousands of years before lovers find
that what they really sought was in their own souls". When all
the "broken lights" are seen to be reflections of the One Light,
the One Beloved, we shall know the great Unity of which the
mystics speak, and we shall know the separate myriad forms
for what they are.

10

Learning from the Opposites

IN HIS BOOK THE *Human Situation*, W. MACNEILE DIXON QUOTES
a sonnet by Blanco White, which I have always recalled with
pleasure since I read it some thirty years ago. It is addressed
To Night.

> Mysterious Night! when our first parent knew
> > Thee from report divine, and heard thy name,
> Did he not tremble for this lovely frame,
> > This glorious canopy of light and blue,
> Yet neath a curtain of translucent dew,
> > Bathed in the rays of the great setting flame,
> > Hesperus with the host of heaven came,
> And Lo! Creation widened in man's view.
>
> Who could have thought such darkness lay concealed
> > Within thy beams, O sun, or who could find,
> Whilst flower and leaf and insect stood revealed,
> > That to such countless orbs thou mad'st us blind!
> > Why do we then shun death with anxious strife?
> If Light can thus deceive, wherefore not Life?

The poet, by contrasting Day and Night, is reminding us that
each discloses much that is wonderful, but at the same time,
hides from us what only its opposite can reveal. We know both
the Beauty and the Vastness of creation only when we know
both Day and Night. The same may be true of all the great
Opposites, e.g., Joy and Suffering, Life and Death, etc.

In his biography of *Grey of Fallodon*, G. M. Trevelyan includes

a number of letters Grey wrote to intimate friends, after the
death of his first wife Dorothy. They had enjoyed twenty years
of idyllic happiness together before Dorothy was killed when
the horse drawing her pony-carriage shied at something on a
country-road, and threw her out. In a letter to Katherine
Lyttelton after his bereavement, Grey wrote:

> It is true that I am alone, but in that way I learn what
> sorrow teaches, and that is to the good. For instance, I ask,
> if Dorothy joined me again, should I be more or less loving
> now? And the answer is "more loving". I had learned all
> that happiness could teach me, and now I have learned more,
> *for sorrow and happiness both teach love, only, each leaves so much
> untaught which only the other can give.* And so if I am learning
> and growing, my spirit is becoming more fit to meet hers, or
> to go when the time comes, wherever hers has gone . . . Much
> of each day is very sad. But I am used to that, and before
> each day is over there come thoughts that turn to peace.

Mrs Creighton, a cousin of Dorothy's wrote of her, "I do not
think she would have asked why it (her life) was cut short. She
had too clear a sense of the bigness of things to imagine one
can either understand or explain. She was very reverent where
she could not understand."

In a letter to his friend C. F. Andrews, Tagore the Indian
poet-philosopher writes about the problem of the Opposites,
and in particular about the pair which he called Joy and Pain.
He wrote:

> The Infinite Being is not complete if He remains absolutely
> infinite. He must realise Himself through the finite: i.e.,
> through Creation. The impulse to realize comes from the
> fullness of Joy, but the process must be through pain. You
> cannot ask why it should be, why the Infinite should attain
> Truth by passing through finitude; why the joy should be
> the cause of the suffering to come back to Itself – for it is
> so. And when our minds are illumined, we feel glad that it
> is so.
>
> When we fix all our attention to that side of the Infinite
> where it is pain and death, where it is the process of fulfil-
> ment, we are overwhelmed. But we know that there is the

other side; that there is a completeness along with the in-complete ... Otherwise there would be no pity in us for the suffering; no love in us for the imperfect ... In creation, joy is always getting the better of pain, otherwise, our sym-pathy for pain would be unmeaning. Why should we despair? We cannot fathom the mystery of existence. But this much we have known, that there is a love which in truth is greater than pain and death. Is not that sufficient for us?

I don't think much more can be expressed in words of the mystery of suffering. It can be experienced by the mystic, who, in high moment has known the overwhelming love which the Father has for all His children. All souls carry within them a basic home-sickness, even though, for the majority of people, this has scarcely risen into consciousness. The world of the opposites, which is so much a world of desires, provides the stimulus which galvanises the lower elements in us – body and mind, into action. An attractive, peaceful, perfect world, would not do this, and we should make no effort to get "Home". This is why the heaven-worlds (or astral worlds), are often des-cribed as idyllic. Most of the acute tensions which we know here are absent or minimal on those levels of consciousness: but as a result, the stimuli which make for progress are also less marked.

The seventeenth-century clergyman-poet George Herbert, wrote some quaint verses to which he gave the title *The Pulley*. The term "rest" in his second verse is the equivalent of "peace", while in the fourth verse it is the equivalent of "the others".

When God at first made man,
Having a glass of blessings standing by,
"Let us," said He "pour on him all we can:
Let the world's riches, which disperséd lie
Contract into a span."

So strength first made a way;
Then beauty flowed, then wisdom, honour, pleasure;
When almost all was out, God made a stay,
Perceiving that, alone of all His treasure,
Rest in the bottom lay.

"For if I should," said He,

"Bestow this jewell also on My creature,
He would adore My gifts instead of Me,
And rest in Nature, not the God of Nature:
    So both should losers be.

"Yet let him keep the rest,
But keep them with repining restlessness;
Let him be rich and weary, that at least,
If goodness lead him not, yet weariness
    May toss him to My breast."

Here, we human beings are tossed to and fro by winds of change; by the tension between "I ought" and "I want"; between the soul, – which only longs for God, – and the ego which wants the fulfilment of its own desires. The soul is not looking for a "peace" or "rest" which is the opposite of conflict, but for a higher divine quality of being, by finding which, it can transcend altogether the turmoil of the opposites.

Dr C. G. Jung once expressed the view, "The most important problems of life are all fundamentally insoluble. They must be so, because they express the necessary polarity in every self-regulating system. They can never be solved: they can only be outgrown." The process of outgrowing is acquired through the power to lift consciousness above the level of conflict. He said:

When I examined the way of development of those persons, who quietly, and as if unconsciously, grew beyond themselves, I saw that their fates had something in common. Whether arising from without or from within, the new thing came to all those persons from a dark field of possibilities, and they accepted it . . . I have been deeply impressed by the fact that the new thing prepared by fate seldom or never corresponds to conscious expectation . . . What then did these people do in order to achieve the process that freed them? As far as I can see, they did nothing but *let things happen*.

Dr Jung did not mean by this an attitude of despair, indifference or defeatism, but an attitude of inner acceptance of life. It is an attitude in which there is no resentment or rebellion against God. Nothing *can* happen to us unless God allows it to happen. It is likely to be karmic in its origin and by making a right reaction to it, we grow spiritually and discharge the karma. The "right" reaction is a courageous trusting acceptance. "All things work together for good to those who love God."

> With eager heart and will on fire,
> I fought to win my great desire.
> "Peace shall be mine," I said, but life
> Grew bitter in the weary strife.
>   . . .
> Broken at last, I bowed my head,
> Forgetting all myself, and said,
> "Whatever comes, His will be done,"
> And in that moment, peace was won.
>
>   (Henry van Dyke)

11

Transcending the Opposites

A PATIENT OF DR C. G. JUNG WROTE A LETTER TO HIM, FROM which he has quoted the following passage:

> Out of evil much good has come to me. By keeping quiet, repressing nothing, remaining attentive, and hand in hand with that, by accepting Reality – taking things as they are, and not as I wanted them to be – by doing all this, rare knowledge has come to me, and rare powers as well, such as I could never have imagined before. I always thought that when we accept things, they overpower us in one way or another. Now this is not true at all, and it is only by accepting them that we can define an attitude towards them. So now I intend playing the game of life, being receptive to whatever comes to me, good and bad, sunshine and shadow that are for ever shifting . . .
>
> What a fool I was! How I tried to force everything to go according to my idea!

In one of his letters to his friend C. F. Andrews, Rabindranath Tagore includes a poem which he has translated from the original Bengali into English prose, about "taking truth simply".

> Whatever may come, my heart, take truth simply;
> Though there be some who can love you, there must be
>   others who never can, and if you must know the
>   cause, it is as much in you as in them, and in all
>   things around.

Some doors are closed against your knocks, while your
      doors are not open always, and to all comers.
Such has been and shall be for evermore; and yet, if you
      must have peace, my heart, take truth simply.

There is no need to be abusive if your boat founders by
      the shore though it sailed through the storm.
Keep yourself afloat by all means; but if it is impossible to
      do so, then be good enough to sink without noise.
It is a commonplace fact that things may or may not fit
      you, and events happen without asking for your leave,
Yet if you must have peace, my heart, take truth simply.

You press and are pressed hard in the crowd, but space
      there is enough and to spare in this world.
When you have counted your losses to the last farthing,
      your sky remains as blue as ever.
You find, when suddenly tested, that to live is sweeter than
      to die.
You may miss this and that and the other thing, but if you
      must have peace, my heart, take truth simply.

Must you stand with your back to the rising sun, and
      watch your shadow lengthened before you?*
Must you take pleasure in finding fault with your destiny,
      and thus tease your soul to death?
Then for mercy's sake be quick and have done with it, for
      if, with the evening stars, you must light your lamp,
      my heart, take truth simply.

Here the heart is being addressed, not the mind. The poem
is advocating an acceptance, with humble simplicity of all that
life presents to us. The first verse reflects upon inter-personal
relationships. Its advice is to accept the differences and pre-
ferences which exist, and not try to mould others into any
conformity. The second verse refers to events and suggests
again that the true wisdom is to accept them rather than resent
them. The third verse reminds the heart not to make an adverse
judgment upon life merely because its own difficulties are so
evident. The fourth verse deplores the fault-finders, the shiners

---

*We may allow poetic license; but cannot refrain from observing that with
one's back to the rising sun, the shadows would shorten.

and the grumblers at life, and tells the soul that if it is to return to the stars it must not quarrel with the conditions of existence but accept them. Only thus can it transcend them.

This is one of the basic wisdoms of life. If the law of Karma underlies every event and relationship on this physical level there should be no grounds for resentment. All that we are and all that happens to us derives from what we have created through our long past. In our attitude to it in the present lies the modification of our future karma. A sage* once said, "Man invites his own calamities, and then protests against the irksome guests, having forgotten how, and when, and where, he penned and sent out the invitations. But Time does not forget; and Time delivers, in due season, each invitation to the right address . . ."

If we believe this and live by it, we need not be concerned with success and failure as the world judges of these things, nor with right and wrong (which conventional morality would regard as our directive). We need only ask ourselves, "Have I passed this test or have I failed?" When we look at all the riddles of life: apparent injustices, so-called tragedies, personal entanglements, illnesses, sufferings of the apparently innocent, etc, we can regard everything as reflecting on the physical level a karmic situation which we ourselves created. It offers to the persons involved an opportunity once more to straighten things out, to unravel knots of character, to react rightly, and therefore to free future life or lives from the same entanglements. If we look at surface appearances and stand upon our rights, the ego is almost certainly making the same reaction that it has made scores of times before. An act of self-sacrifice is called for to prevent the karmic spiral plunging more deeply into suffering.

The question might be asked of one's self, "Am I prepared to act in the way that Love and unselfishness indicate to me, or shall I continue to follow the way that my ego will try to drive me?"

Many a person finds difficulty in accepting restriction. Perhaps it is a job which does not offer to a person an adequate opportunity of using the gifts and skills brought to it. Perhaps a person is short of money, and feels unable to do all the

* *The Book of Mirdad*, Mikhail Naimy (Stuart & Watkins).

desirable things which he would like to do, if only things were different. How confident the ego is that it could improve vastly on the blue-print of life! There is no virtue in restriction itself, so that its occurrence must be accepted as a testing of character, and therefore as another opportunity given to us to progress. The way through is surely to recognise that we can eliminate a weakness in our character and discharge a karmic debt. Why postpone what ultimately we have to face? We may discharge the situation for ever, by accepting it, and even blessing it. The over-ruling Karmic Powers are then free to change it.

In *The Initiate in the new World* by Cyril Scott, a Master replies to a disciple who has asked him to heal some disability, "When you have learned to ignore it, and work as efficiently as though you hadn't got it, I'll put you on to a cure ... My son, it is a greater achievement to do good work in spite of a sick body, than to cure the body itself."

A second illustration occurs in the New Testament story of the Man born blind, who was healed by Jesus. The disciples afterwards asked their Master, "Lord, who did sin, this man or his parents, that he should be born blind?" The reply of Jesus is said to have been, "Neither did this man sin, nor his parents, that he was born blind; but that the works of God should be manifest in him. I must work the works of Him that sent me." For many years I was puzzled by this answer. If neither the man himself nor his parents were responsible for his being *born* blind, presumably this rules out a karmic origin. It surely cannot mean that this man had suffered from blindness throughout his life merely to provide the occasion for a remarkable miracle of healing? Now I see that Jesus was telling His disciples that this man's soul *chose* to be born in a blind body, because it knew what spiritual gain would accrue from this, and because it knew that because of this he would meet the Master face to face. George Russell (A.E.) wrote:

I feel that in some secrecy of our being, we are the choosers: that we willed what we have done. Even if the outer being finds itself outcast, in prison, hopeless or suffering, the inner spirit knew what wisdom or power it would have through understanding such things ... Before we are reborn, we may, as Plato suggests, choose the circumstances of our lives ...

If we find ourselves miserable or helpless here, we are not condemned to that pain by a deity outside ourselves.

> I thank Thee too, that Thou hast made
>   Joy to abound,
> So many gentle thoughts and deeds
>   Circling us round,
> That in the darkest spot of earth
>   Some love is found.
>
> I thank Thee more than all our joy
>   Is touched with pain,
> That shadows fall on brightest hours,
>   That thorns remain,
> So that earth's bliss may be our guide,
>   And not our chain.
>
> I thank Thee Lord, that Thou hast kept
>   The best in store;
> We have enough, yet not too much
>   To long for more –
> A yearning for a deeper peace
>   Not known before.
>
>   (Adelaide A. Proctor)

12

Reflections on Prayer and Meditation

IS THERE ANY WESTERN SEEKER AFTER THINGS OF THE SPIRIT WHO
has not, at some moments of his life shared the burden of
Wordsworth's lament:

> The world is too much with us; late and soon,
> Getting and spending, we lay waste our powers;
> Little we see in Nature that is ours;
> We have given our hearts away, a sordid boon!

Wordsworth managed however to keep so close to Nature
that far more characteristically, he could write:

> ... from the naked top
> Of some bold headland, he beheld the sun
> Rise up and bathe the world in light! He looked –
> Ocean and earth, the solid frame of earth
> And ocean's liquid mass in gladness lay
> Beneath him: – Far and wide the clouds were touched,
> And in their silent faces could be read
> Unutterable love. Sound needed none,
> Nor any voice of joy; his spirit drank
> The spectacle; sensation, soul, and form,
> All melted into him; they swallowed up
> His animal being; in them did he live,
> And by them did he live; they were his life.
> In such access of mind, in such high hour
> Of visitation from the living God,
> Thought was not; in enjoyment it expired.

No thanks he breathed, he proffered no request;
Rapt into still communion that transcends
The imperfect offices of prayer and praise,
His mind was a thanksgiving to the power
That made him; it was blessedness and love!

In this experience, through the translucent sensitivity of the poet's mind the outer and inner worlds moved towards unity (a unity which in fact they have – but which the mind cleaves in two). We may expect to find the Spirit outside us when we have uncovered the eye of the Soul and touched the Spirit within us. Meditation is the way to approach this.

What is meant by meditation? Everyone is familiar with the commonplace state of "busy-mindedness" in which one thought after another flits across the screen of awareness. In another simile, the mind has been likened to a lake, the surface of which is constantly subject to ripples of thought. Meditation is a discipline which brings the restless mind to rest, and when this can be properly achieved the clear depths of the lake which were hitherto obscured, slowly reveal themselves. Expressed in another metaphor, the mind of man, ruled by the ego, is saturated with self-interest (both coarse and refined) and is a dark overcast sky which cuts off the lower levels of ourselves from the divine sunshine of the Soul which like the sun, is always shining. Most men therefore live under clouded skies a sad, dull, confused, and rather meaningless existence. We might say that the object of meditation is to break through this cloud layer and finally to disperse it altogether, so that at last we come to realise that we *are* the immortal soul through which the divine light is shining. With even a partial break-through life starts to change slowly. It loses much of its turbulence and meaninglessness, and there is a radiation of divine peace instead.

Even on a short-term view meditation each day is a rewarding activity, but its long-term objective is to allow the soul to rule the life, to know Itself, and therefore to know God. This is called by Christian mystics the Illumined state. Between the first glimpse of light and the full sunshine of the Spirit lies the long journey and disciplines of the Spiritual Path. These disciplines are referred to by St Francis in his famous prayer:

Lord, make me an instrument of Thy peace:
Where there is hatred let me sow love;
When I am injured may I forgive,
Where there is doubt may I bring faith,
Where there is despair may I bring hope,
Where there is darkness may I bring light,
Where there is sadness may I bring joy.

Grant, O Lord,
Not that I may be comforted, but that I may comfort,
Not that I may be understood, but that I may understand,
Not that I may be loved, but that I may love.
For he who gives to others receives.
He who forgives others is himself forgiven,
And he who dies to himself awakens to Eternal Life.

One who meditates with the aim of reaching up to God, knows without being told that his love for God and God's Love for him will sustain him to the end of his journey. A Master once said to his disciples, "Meditation is a love-affair between your soul and the Heavenly Father." We have to *yearn* to know God, and be ready if necessary to let all else go. (But in reality, there is nothing else but God.)

Purification is an important discipline, for no-one could expect to draw any nearer to the Holy Presence while holding on to the dross and dirt of inner uncleanness. It would be helpful to sit quietly from time to time deliberately to look-in at the more hidden levels of ourselves, in order to know what we are really like, what purification from selfishness means for us, and how we can best contend with our weaknesses. Slowly, on the Path, a change sets in which involves a change in our values. We have been hitherto conditioned by generally accepted or traditional values; these must be brought to the bar of the soul's own judgment. Often these habit-tracks run so deep that more lives than one are needed to overcome the restrictions and limitations and prejudices. (To know God means complete freedom from any imposed restrictions.)

Francis Thompson was clearly aware of all this when he wrote in *The Mistress of Vision*:

Pierce thy heart to find the key:
With thee take
Only what none else would keep;
Learn to dream when thou dost wake,
Learn to wake when thou dost sleep.
Learn to water joy with tears,
Learn from fears to vanquish fears;
To hope, for thou dar'st not despair;
Exult, for that thou dar'st not grieve;
Plough thou the rock until it bear;
Know, for thou else could'st not believe;
Lose that the lost thou may'st receive;
Die, for none other way can'st live.
When earth and heaven lay down their veil,
And that apocalypse turns thee pale;
When thy seeing blindeth thee
To what thy fellow-mortals see;
When their sight to thee is sightless;
Their living, death; their light, most lightless;
Search no more –
Pass the gates of Luthany, tread the region Elenore.

Summing up in simple language, this means no emotional attachment to persons and things of this life; a rising above 'wanting' or 'desiring' for the self; and an acceptance of what comes by trusting in God ("Thy will be done"). This is a great spiritual achievement.

I find that prayer can sometimes be the best gateway into meditation. It may be the only possible way if mind and emotions are disturbed and unruly. In the simplicity of child-like prayer the mind can become unburdened and surrender a situation to the all-loving will of the Heavenly Father. He is both all-Loving and all-Knowing, so that the words we use are to unburden ourselves, – not to give Him information. When peace descends, all that may linger in such prayer is "God . . . God . . . God" and even this may die away into a Peace which passes understanding.

Shelley, whose sensitive and compassionate mind was oppressed by "doubt, chance, and mutability" neven found the key which would have set him gloriously free in spirit. In his *Hymn to Intellectual Beauty* are found the following lines:

Thy light alone – like mists o'er mountains driven,
    Or music by the night-wind sent
    Through strings of some still instrument
    Or moonlight on a midnight stream,
Gives grace and truth to life's unquiet dream.

If we use them to address the Eternal Light, these lines describe the blessings which can come to those who meditate – even though the Goal is still far distant.

13

Passers-By

IN THE UNCANONICAL GOSPEL ACCORDING TO THOMAS, IT IS recorded that Jesus once said, "Learn to become passers-by." It rings true to His spirit. He once said to those around Him, "Foxes have holes and the birds of the air have nests, but the Son of Man hath not where to lay his head." For three crowded years He moved constantly from one place to another, healing the sick, teaching those who were hungry to find meaning in life, and initiating on to the Divine Path those who had reached a point where they could begin to climb the Mountain of God. Having spiritually taken these as far as He could, and aware that His mission was now complete (except for the climactic event of the Crucifixion), He prepared to face this and return to His Father's Kingdom.

In St John's Gospel, (12:20–26), there is an intriguing account of certain Greeks who asked one of the disciples for an interview with Jesus. Did they proffer to Him an invitation to visit Greece and teach there? The records do not tell us, but it seems significant that immediately following their visit, Jesus uttered those moving and memorable words which have been an inspiration to gallant self-sacrificing souls all down the ages:

"Except a grain of wheat fall into the ground and die, it abideth alone; but if it die, it beareth much fruit. He that loveth his life loseth it, but he that hateth his life in this world shall keep it unto life eternal. Whoever wants to serve Me must follow Me." Humanly speaking, it looks as though the alternatives before Him were further work and teaching in Greece, or crucifixion at the hands of the Jews. He chose the latter because He saw it was the Father's will.

"Learn to become passers-by." There have always been ascetics and hermits who have adopted an attitude of world-negation and withdrawal from human life. Neither by teaching nor example did Jesus adopt this position. While withdrawing from the active round of things for meditation and prayer, He used to the full His opportunity to move among men and women in service. With inner knowledge (like all great Masters), He then chose the time of His departure.

Mankind, which knows nothing of the Spiritual Path, over-values the physical order. It is, after all, the only level which is disclosed to the senses of the physical body, and most men are conditioned by this. There are however, innumerable levels of consciousness and realms of being, far higher and more satisfying than the physical one. These beckon to the pilgrim-soul to move on. "Learn to become passers-by." It is the spirit which these words embody which led the Sufi poet Abul Fazi to write, "Jesus, on Whom be peace, said, 'The world is a bridge. Pass over it, but build no house upon it'." This is written on the Mosque of Akbar at Fateh pur Sikri in India.

To be a passer-by is to practise the great (and often hard) teaching about detachment. The spiritual pilgrim must be willing to "Walk on" and not "Hold on". Perhaps this thought motivated W. B. Yeats when he wrote the epitaph for his own tombstone, "Cast a cold eye on life, on death. Horseman, pass by!" It is the same insight which William Blake expressed in the verse:

> He who bends to himself a Joy
> Doth the wingèd life destroy;
> But he who kisses the Joy as it flies
> Lives in Eternity's sunrise.

For countless lives the ego has sought the fulfilment of its own desires. I like this thing; I want that thing (or person); I crave security; I covet that opportunity, and so on. We desire, we obtain, and we hold on to persons, possessions, power, and that which has passed. If we are attempting the Spiritual Path all this is holding us back. On this Path nothing is essential except our will to persevere. We may have to be prepared to let everything go and trust in God as our only Security. If he is perfect Love, can we not trust Him? "Learn to become passers-by." The Buddha was very moved by the impermanence of all around, and he too taught this wisdom.

Human life has been so frequently described as a journey or a pilgrimage. John Bunyan, the immortal tinker, who spent many years of his life in Bedford gaol, wrote of life in these courageous terms:

Who would true valour see,
　Let him come hither;
One here will constant be.
　Come wind, come weather;
There's no discouragement
Shall make him once relent
His first avowed intent
　To be a pilgrim.

Who so beset him round
　With dismal stories
Do but themselves confound;
　His strength the more is.
No lion can him fright,
He'll with a giant fight,
But he will have a right
　To be a pilgrim.

Hobgoblin nor foul fiend
　Can daunt his spirit:
He knows he at the end
　Shall life inherit.
Then fancies fly away;
He'll fear not what men say
He'll labour night and day
　To be a pilgrim.

Recalling "glorious" seventeenth century England, with its literary, scientific and geographical expansion, it was a time of black horrors, appalling cruelty, widespread superstition, and medieval theology. James I caused an Act to be passed which made it a capital offence "to remove or conjure up an evil spirit, to consult with, or feed one; to use magic or to hinder cattle by means of charms". Before Bunyan died, more than

70,000 people in England were martyred under this Act. When Charles II came to the throne, a new act of parliament made it an offence to preach without a licence. For this, John Bunyan was thrown into gaol for twelve years. He was a good man, and however restricted his theological outlook may appear today, people knew he was a good and sincere man and listened to him. In prison, the thought of his suffering family tortured him, and he spent much time making shoe-laces to keep them from destitution. He knew that his little blind daughter Mary, of whom he was very fond, would have to sell these shoe laces or beg for a living. The decision cost him great conflict and emotion, but he said to himself, "Yet, I must do it." When he finally came out of prison he bore no bitterness or resentment, but had an inner peace which many in our modern world would envy. As readers of *The Pilgrim's Progress* know, John Bunyan puts into the mouth of one of his characters Mr Valiant-for-Truth, words which might fittingly be applied to their author, as he came to the end of his own life-pilgrimage at sixty.

When he understood it, he called for his friends and told them of it. Then, said he, I am going to my Father's; and though with great difficulty I have got hither, yet now I do not repent me of all the troubles I have been at to arrive where I am. My sword I give to him who shall succeed me in my pilgrimage, and my courage and skill to him who can get it. My marks and scars I carry with me, to be a witness to me that I have fought His battles, Who will now be my rewarder.

When the day was come that he must go hence, many accompanied him to the riverside . . . So he passed over, and all the trumpets sounded for him on the other side.

When Winston Churchill characteristically planned in advance the detailed pageantry of his commemoration service in St Paul's Cathedral, London, John Bunyan's hymn was one of two which he chose as appropriate to the occasion. To me the choice was rather moving, and I smiled at the irony of princes and potentates of worldly fame singing the words of the immortal tinker who spent twelve years of his life in Bedford Gaol. Churchill and Bunyan are to the worldly eye poles apart. One presided over Britain's destiny at a most critical time in its history; the other suffered in prison at a time when freedom in

Britain was at a low ebb. One was an aristocrat, and the Queen's First Minister; the other was a poor man and a victim of the Establishment. But they had important things in common. Each of them fought for freedom in his own way. Neither could be daunted by what seemed overwhelming odds. Both were men of integrity, and both were men of outstanding valour. Both wrote magnificent English, and both won immortal names. Both were men of compassion. Attlee speaks of a visit that he and Churchill made to a south country town soon after a fearful bombing. He relates how the sight of a little home and shop exposed by the blown-out walls brought tears to Churchill's eyes, and he said, "We've got to do something about that damage *now*." Within twenty-four hours plans were set in motion for a committee to deal with such things, and this subsequently became the War Damages Commission.

It is pleasant to think that when Britain stood for a time alone against Hitler, Churchill may have sometimes reflected on Bunyan's verse:

> Who so beset him round
>   With dismal stories,
> Do but themselves confound;
>   His strength the more is.
> No lion can him fright,
> He'll with a giant fight,
> But he will have a right
>   To be a pilgrim.

What has Bunyan's hymn to say to *us*?

"Who would true valour see, let him come hither." It is a reminder that the Spiritual Path is not for cowards or for the faint-hearted. It requires valour and the trust which refuses to be dismayed by odds. It offers the pilgrim a supreme assurance – the only one that matters – "One here will constant be, come wind, come weather." The Divine constancy is the pilgrim's one security when the winds of change are blowing hard, when the climbing is difficult, and when familiar landmarks are being obscured or swept away. Yet, as the great Master of Galilee said, "No man having set his hand to the plough and looking back, is fit for the Kingdom of God." The hymn says this also:

There's no discouragement
Shall make him once relent
His first avowed intent
   To be a pilgrim.

It may be that for modern man the possibility of meeting
"hobgoblins" or "foul fiends" creates no serious concern.
On the Spiritual Path, these terms appropriately describe the
selfish ego-centre with which the soul of man has to do constant
battle. It is a battle which is never won until the Gates of the
Kingdom are reached and the threshold is crossed. To reach the
end of this, – the greatest journey in the world, – the pilgrim
has to "labour night and day", and has to "care not what men
say".

Courage! my friend: when the way looks difficult and gloomy
for you. Others have travelled the same way successfully, and
by their trust and their courage they have won through.

Does the road wind uphill all the way?
   Yes, to the very end.
Will the day's journey take the whole long day?
   From morn to night, my friend.

But is there for the night a resting-place?
   A roof for when the slow dark hours begin.
May not the darkness hide it from my face?
   You cannot miss the inn.

Shall I meet other wayfarers at night?
   Those who have gone before.
Then must I knock, or call when just in sight?
   They will not keep you standing at the door.

Shall I find comfort, travel-sore and weak?
   Of labour you shall find the sum.
Will there be beds for me and all who seek?
   Yea, beds for all who come.
                              (Christina Rossetti)

14

The Way, The Truth and The Life

JESUS, WHO HAS BEEN DESCRIBED AS "THE MASTER OF MASTERS", once made a remarkable claim. He said to His disciples, "I am the Way, the Truth and the Life." He was not then speaking of Himself as the finite historic figure who walked on the roads of Palestine two thousand years ago, but as the Voice and embodiment of the Christ-consciousness. Whatever term is used – the Christ-consciousness, the Word, the Logos, the Light within the Soul – it rules all those Beings who are En-lightened. The Christ-consciousness is the Goal of us all. The Way to reach this goal is shown to us by the Enlightened Ones, and through their grace is given the Life which is necessary if we are to travel along the Way.

Alice Meynell wrote a short poem portraying the pilgrim-soul addressing the Christ-Spirit:

> Thou art the Way.
> Hadst Thou been nothing but the Goal,
>   I cannot say
> If Thou hadst ever met my soul.
>
>   I cannot see –
> I, child of process, – if there lies
>   An end for me,
> Full of repose, full of replies.
>
>   I'll not reproach
> The road that winds, my feet that err,
>   Access, Approach,
> Art Thou, Time, Way, and Wayfarer.

In the first verse the Way and the Goal are seen related as means and end. Had the Christ-consciousness been only the splendid goal of Man's aspiration, – a perfect state at present far beyond him – would man have even dared to hope that he could reach it? Every traveller on the Spiritual Path knows the impossibility of climbing the mountain of God unaided. The ego would be an insuperable drag, and the Goal would remain unattempted – "the highest for earth too high". It is a matter for the deepest gratitude that Enlightened Ones come from time to time to our world-level to show us the way Home.

The second verse is the very human – and intellectual – reaction to the Spiritual Path. We may be no longer restricted by the life of the valleys where we once felt at home, but we do not feel acclimatised to the path of ascent, and we hesitate in the rarified air of the upward way. We question and we wonder. We cannot see the summit from where we are: we cannot even be sure that it can be reached. Shall we trust and walk on? Or shall we give away the tremendous effort, – for this life-time at least?

The third verse gives the only possible reply of the soul which has once glimpsed the summit, even though the clouds have come down again. "I'll not reproach the road that winds, my feet that err. Access, Approach, art Thou; Time, Way, and Wayfarer." The content of this affirmation is the ground for our trust and optimism: that the Christ-consciousness is from time to time embodied as *Wayfarer*. The Word becomes flesh and dwells among us. He is an ever-present Help who travels the road with us, helping us over the dangerous places and guiding us over the ice-falls. Men would have no hope of climbing the Mountain of God, were it not for Enlightened Ones who leave the bliss of their own spiritual country to help us back to where they have come from. Moses and Buddha, Nanak and Kabir, Krishna and Jesus, Ramana and many another have been Wayfarers for our sakes, and how much we owe to them! Few things are more moving than to meditate upon the self-sacrifice and descent of these great souls, in order to help us along. Ramakrishna died in 1886 at the age of fifty, of cancer of the throat. Ramana Maharshi died in 1950 from a cancer. Jesus chose to go to a painful torturing death by crucifixion. Have we ever reflected that it was not their own karma to do this, but it was the karma of others which they chose to carry?

They did this voluntarily to give others with heavy karmic debts a spiritual opportunity which otherwise they would not have had in this life. The burdens they carried were the last gifts of great Masters to those who were dear to them. They were the Wayfarers, of each of Whom it could be said, "He was bruised for our iniquities; the chastisement of our peace was upon Him, and with His stripes, we are healed."

> . . . Souls tempered with fire,
> Fervent, heroic, and good,
> Helpers and friends of mankind.
>
> Servants of God! or sons
> Shall I not call you? because
> Not as servants ye knew
> Your father's innermost mind,
> His, who unwillingly sees
> One of his little ones lost –
> Yours is the praise, if mankind
> Hath not as yet in its march
> Fainted, and fallen, and died!
>
>   . . .
>
> Beacons of hope, ye appear!
> Langour is not in your heart,
> Weakness is not in your word,
> Weariness not on your brow.
> Ye alight in our van; at your voice,
> Panic, despair, flee away.
> Ye move through the ranks, recall
> The stragglers, refresh the outworn,
> Praise, re-inspire the brave.
> Order, courage, return.
> Eyes rekindling, and prayers,
> Follow your steps as ye go.
> Ye fill up the gaps in our files,
> Strengthen the wavering line,
> Stablish, continue our march
> On, to the bound of the waste
> On, to the City of God.
>
>   (Matthew Arnold)

A Master once said to His disciples: "The only reason you have for this journey is to meet One who can take you Home. There are no reasons for sorrow, anxiety, discouragement, or despair. I can take you to the Light . . . open the door and let Love in."

Quoting from two other poets who were sensitive to the heavy load carried by these great Servants of Humanity, first from A. E. (George Russell) a poem called *To One Consecrated*:

> The Mighty Mother made you wise,
> Gave love that clears the hidden ways;
> Her glooms were glory to your eyes,
> Her darkness but the fount of days.
>
> She made all gentleness in you
> And beauty radiant as the morn's:
> She made our joy in yours, then drew
> Upon your brow a crown of thorns.
>
> Your eyes are filled with tender light
> For those whose eyes are dim with tears:
> They see your brow is crowned and bright
> But not its rings of wounding spears.

The second poet is Robert Browning, and the poem is called *Saul*.

> As Thy love is discovered almighty, almight be proved
> Thy power, that exists with and for it, of being Beloved!
> He who did most shall bear most; the strongest shall stand
>   the most weak.
> 'Tis the weakness in strength that I cry for! my flesh that
>   I seek
> In the Godhead! I seek and I find it. O Saul, it shall be
> A Face like my face that receives thee; a Man like to me,
> Thou shalt love and be loved by for ever: a Hand like this
>   hand
> Shall throw open the gates of new life to thee! See the
>   Christ stand.

15

Homesickness

THE EARLY YEARS OF HUMAN LIFE ARE EXTRAORDINARILY POWERFUL
in the influences they leave behind which mould the years of
after-life. I shall always be grateful for something indefinable
which was given to me as a boy living at Whitby. This quaint
fishing-town on the Yorkshire coast faces the stormy waves
of the North Sea. During the winter storms, sea-spume blows
inland at high tide, and a fog-horn on the East Cliff warns
shipping of the dangerous coast. The River Esk, which has
gathered its waters out of moorland streams and valleys flows
through woodland and pasture to the harbour and the sea. For
two months in the summer season holiday makers invade the
town, and then the simplicity of life surges back again. The
ruins of St Hilda's Abbey on the East Cliff have brooded for
centuries over the town and have seen the spoilation of Saxon,
Dane and Norseman. Over its daily life around the harbour
dotted with fishing cobbles and larger trawlers is the plaintive
crying of the sea-gulls. It was not until many years later that
I realised I had absorbed unconsciously a great love of this
green countryside, especially where it links the heather-clad
moorlands with the sea. I find that the cries of seagulls wherever
heard, will carry me back over the haze of years to those distant
scenes of my boyhood.

Eva Gore-Booth must have felt a deep affinity for a bit of the
Irish coast when she wrote:

The grand road from the mountain goes shining to the sea,
 And there is traffic in it, and many a horse and cart;
But the little roads of Cloonagh are dearer far to me,

And the little roads of Cloonagh go rambling through
    my heart.

A great storm from the ocean goes shouting o'er the hill,
    And there is glory in it and terror on the wind;
But the haunted air of twilight is very strange and still,
    And the little winds of twilight are dearer to my mind.

The great waves of the Atlantic sweep storming on their way,
    Shining green and silver with the hidden herring shoal;
But the little waves of Breffny have drenched my heart in
    spray
    And the little waves of Breffny go stumbling through
      my soul.

Robert Louis Stevenson wrote of his childhood home in
Scotland with nostalgic memories:

Fire and the windows bright glittered on the moorland;
    Song, tuneful song, built a palace in the wild.
Now, when day dawns on the brow of the moorland,
    Lone stands the house, and the chimney-stone is cold.
Lone let it stand, now the friends are all departed
    The kind hearts, the true hearts, that loved the place of
      old.
Spring shall come, come again, calling up the moor-fowl,
    Spring shall bring the sun and rain, bring the bees and
      flowers;
Red shall the heather bloom over hill and valley,
    Soft flow the stream through the even-flowing hours;
Fair the day shine as it shone on my childhood –
    Fair shine the day on the house with open door;
Birds come and cry there and twitter in the chimney –
    But I go for ever and come again no more.

I suspect that this home-sickness, whatever form it takes, has
roots which go deeper into our true nature than can be ac-
counted for by the experiences of the early years of this life.
There is a home-sickness of the soul for its own country, and
every time it ventures again into incarnation with all its grievous
restrictions, it is with the renewed hope that *this* time it will win
the guerdon of immortality. Quoting the words of A. E., "The

fallen divinity for an instance forgets that it is fallen, and speaks as to immortals. There is as great a mystery about our least motion as there is about our whole being." The awakened soul yearns to get Home, as the Prodigal Son did in the parable.

Nostalgia for our childhood's setting is an expression of these powerful emotions: then we were secure with our father and mother, then we had no load of responsibility; neither did the past weigh us down, nor did the future cloud our outlook with apprehension; above all, we were loved. This setting is a microcosm of that for which the soul yearns, and speaks of as the Kingdom of God. "Except ye become as little children," said Jesus, "ye cannot enter the Kingdom."

> Too great Thy heart is to despise,
> Whose day girds centuries about;
> From things which we name small, Thine eyes
> See great things looking out.
>
> I think that nothing made is lost;
> That not a moon has ever shone,
> That not a cloud mine eyes hath crossed,
> But to my soul is gone
> . . .
> That all the lost years garnered lie
> In this Thy casket, my dim soul;
> And Thou wilt once, the key apply
> And show the shining whole.
>
> Father, in joy, our knees we bow:
> This earth is not a place of tombs:
> We are but in the nursery now;
> They in the upper rooms.
>
> For are we not at home in Thee,
> And all this world a visioned show;
> That, knowing what Abroad is, we
> What Home is too may know.

The poem of George MacDonald from which these verses are taken, is called *A Prayer for the Past*. The last verse embodies a philosophy of existence upon which we might deeply meditate. When we try to grasp the meaning of life with our intellect, we soon become painfully aware of how little we *can* know. We

fall back on parables, myths and allegories to help us towards
the right kind of orientation. We cannot hope to have much
more until we reach Illumination. Then there unfolds to the
aspirant those eternal Mysteries which words cannot express
or encompass. The factor of Time alone, is a most grievous
limitation. The reference to human experience as "a visioned
show" is suggestive. Suppose the parable of the Prodigal Son
had been presented as a vivid dream that occurred to the
younger son, the close of this parable in Luke 15 might have
read as follows:

And he awoke from his vivid dream, amazed and troubled,
and said to his elder brother, 'Where am I?'. His brother
replied, 'You are where you have always been. You're at
home, but you've been asleep for a few minutes'. 'But what a
difference!' said the awakening man, slowly coming round.
'I am really quite different from the person I was before I
went to sleep. I went to sleep in ignorance: I have awakened
with knowledge. Now I know myself; I know you; I know my
Father, – and I understand everything. Before the dream I
was asleep. The dream seemed to me to cover a long time, –
but it has awakened me up – for ever.'

In His aspect of Creator, the Almighty may be regarded as
the Author of a great drama. By His imagining, He created all
realms and all creatures in all the levels of being. At first it
existed for Him alone, just as a human drama exists at first only
in the artist's imagination. Then He gave it independent existence or a life of its own, and His power sustains and preserves
this. At a later stage He gave some of the creatures self-
consciousness, so that they know they are alive and conscious.
Men have begun to seek for these meanings and learned of them
from the Illumined Ones who have been on earth and taught
the race.

It has been said that the universe exists for the benefit of souls.
A. E. who always had wise things to say about the great questions,
once put two questions to his soul and received the answers:
  "What is the meaning and end of life here?"
  "Our spring and our summer are an unfolding into light and
form, and our autumn and winter are a fading into the infinite
soul."

"To what end is this life poured forth and withdrawn?"

"The end is creation, and creation is joy. The One awakens out of quiescence as we come forth, and knows Itself in us; as we return we enter It in gladness knowing ourselves."

16

The Consecration of Action

HOW MUCH OF OUR WESTERN KIND OF LIVING IS SPENT IN *DOING*
things. We may call this action, work or duty. It is a state of
constant busyness which we contrast with rest or idleness. The
average Westerner is caught in some routine and has become a
slave to the great machine of civilisation, just as fully as
conquered people in past centuries were enslaved and used by
their captors. If the situation of the ordinary person is anal-
ysed, it has to be admitted that (i) Much of the work done is
dull and monotonous and not creative, (ii) It is undertaken for
remuneration because "a man has to live". (iii) Satisfaction or
pleasure have to be sought for largely outside of these duties.
A minority of people manage to reconcile themselves to the
slave-situation, because it offers a field for their ambition and
power-drives to operate.

When an individual soul begins to awaken and ask questions,
particularly when for many past lives the ego has pursued
pleasure and power in many forms, – and been at last disil-
lusioned by them, there arises a profound discontent with the
world. A person asks, "To what end?" "What's the use?" "Is
anything worthwhile?" The discovery has to be made by each
individual, that until we accept this life as a training-school
for the soul, as a means only to a sublime end, which is knowledge of, and union with God, we shall not find peace of either
heart or mind. We may discover however that if work is done as
unselfish service, i.e., offered wholly to God, – this will minister
to the growth of character. Where it is done for the satisfaction
of the ego-self it makes no contribution to the soul's progress.
George Herbert expresses this in his poem *The Elixir*.

Teach me, my God and King,
    In all things Thee to see,
And what I do in anything
    To do it as for Thee.

A man that looks on glass
    On it may stay his eye;
Or if he pleaseth, through it pass
    And then the heaven espy.

All may of Thee partake:
    Nothing can be so mean
Which with this tincture, "for Thy sake"
    Will not grow bright and clean.

A servant with this clause
    Makes drudgery divine
Who sweeps a room as for thy laws
    Makes that and th'action fine.

This is the famous stone
    That turneth all to gold;
For that which God doth touch and own
    Cannot for less be told.

It is unthinkable that God cares more for a bishop than for a boot-maker, for a man who makes sermons rather than soap. All service ranks the same with God, but the motive behind the service, and the love that shines through the server, – these alone matter to Him.

It is broadly true to say that the West has attached far too much importance to *doing*, at the expense of *being*. Character has been allowed to take care of itself. In the Indian tradition the tendency has been the reverse. Both extreme positions are at fault. If *being* is stressed too much, men tend to withdraw from the world, and in so doing disregard the word of a great Master Who said, "Inasmuch as ye have done it unto the least of these, ye have done it unto Me." Those around us, in need of our help, succour or love, are offering us our greatest opportunity to give selfless service. If we are blind to this because we are lacking in love, we cannot expect to make spiritual progress.

If doing is stressed too much, we have a blindness which cannot see beyond the world of the senses and imagines that an ideal world would be an economic or political Utopia here on this level.

If Love is the ruling principle by which we live our life, we shall neither separate from the world nor be imprisoned in it. We shall live inwardly in constant communion with the Divine Presence, and express this quality of life outwardly in selfless service to others. We shall be in the world, yet not of it.

Here are two thoughts which are worthy of our meditation:

"The right relation between prayer and action is not that conduct is all-important and prayer helps it, but that prayer is all-important and conduct tests it." (Archbishop Temple.)

"You live that you may learn to love; you love that you may learn to live. No other lesson is required of man." (*The Book of Mirdad* by Mikhail Naimy.)

One of the most impressive assessments of the outer life of action in relationship to the inner life of being, is found in the early chapters of the Gita, where Krishna is speaking to his disciple Arjuna.

> The level which is attained by wisdom is attained by right action as well. He who perceives that the two are one, knows the truth . . .
>
> He who dedicates his actions to the Spirit, without any personal attachment to them, he is no more tainted by sin than the water-lily is wetted by water . . .
>
> Having abandoned the fruit of action, he wins eternal peace.
>
> Others acquainted with spirituality, led by desire, and clinging to the benefit which they think will follow their actions, become entangled by them.

The things that we do in the external world are necessarily impermanent: they create their karma, if our ego was responsible for them, and these consequences have to be met. In contrast, the quality of character that we build is enduring, and this is carried with us on all levels of attainment.

On the physical level, we are all involved in action to some extent. To maintain our life we have to be concerned with food, clothing and shelter, although views on what is considered a desirable minimum may differ widely. Perhaps the most fortunate life is one in which there is sufficient of these necessities to avoid concern about possessing them, but not so much as to introduce concern about preserving them. We cannot all be fortunate in this respect, and without doubt, both wealth and poverty can be severe tests of character.

So much of worldly life is illustrated by the story of a visitor talking to a farmer. The visitor said to him, "What do you use the horses for?" The farmer replied, "To plough the fields." "What are you ploughing the fields for?" said the visitor. "To sow oats," said the farmer. "And what do you do with the oats?" the visitor asked. "We feed the horses," said the farmer. The story may be apocryphal, but does it not describe the intrinsic character of most worldly activity? What *are* we living for? Does it satisfy us to suppose that there is any great merit or value in keeping the complex mechanism of civilised society going? This is merely doing what billions of others have done since the planet first supported human life, and billions of others will doubtless continue to do the same thing. What about all the unfulfilled longings, the sadness and suffering, the heartache and tragedy? Few people whom I have questioned would like to go through the experience of their life again. Let us relentlessly cut through all superficial judgments of life if we really seek to know the answer to the question, "What are we living for?"

However reluctant many awakening souls may be to return to physical embodiment, they know deep down that it is a privilege to have a physical body where it is possible to meet and discharge physical karma of the past. Thus they tear away the veils of illusion and spiritual ignorance. God has to be fully realised and truly known while living on the physical level in order to win freedom from the wheel of births and deaths. Have we got our sense of values correct or are we relegating the inner life to a subsidiary place? The approach to God is all-important, and outer activity, which involves our relationships with our fellows, helps us to see what inner progress we are making. I often reflect on a sentence which A.E. wrote in a letter to a friend who had been urging him to seek a position of wider influence than the one he held. "My friend, a man's success or failure is always with his own soul."

To those who are aspiring towards the Spiritual Path, or who are walking along it, we can affirm without hesitation that our living must put first and foremost the Kingdom of God. All else

will then fall into place. If we resolve to put God's will first –
not our own – action will be always God's activity performed
through us. Success and failure in the accepted sense, will not be
our concern. We are loving to others because we ourselves are
so much loved by the Father. We live from day to day, trusting
the Father, and offering every moment of our lives to Him.

17

On Doing one's own Duty

IN THE COURSE OF HIS TEACHING TO ARJUNA, LORD KRISHNA (an embodiment of the Christ-consciousness), makes the following statement, "It is better to do thine own duty, however lacking in merit, than to do that of another even though efficiently. It is better to die doing one's own duty, for to do the duty of another is fraught with danger."

There are occasions when we are tempted to think, "If only I was in *that* situation instead of *this* one; if only I had those gifts and abilities instead of my own! If only . . ." We forget so easily that the karma that comes to us is our own creation, and the opportunity to meet it is offered to us at the right time. To crave another's opportunity is to be short-sighted, attaching importance to external achievement, and forgetting that nothing happens by chance.

How little do we see of the past pattern of lives, and why things are as they are! Indian teaching has a useful term "dharma" which embodies the concept of one's duty and one's life-pattern. Personal dharma is that which one is called upon to fulfil, because by so doing it is the opportunity provided for one's maximum spiritual unfolding. T. E. Brown's poem *Opifex* seems to me an expression of this idea.

> As I was carving images from clouds,
>> And tinting them with soft ethereal dyes
>> Pressed from the pulp of dreams, one comes and cries:
> "Forbear!" and all my heaven with gloom enshrouds.
>
> "Forbear!" Thou hast no tools wherewith to essay

The delicate waves of that elusive grain:
Wouldst have due recompense of vulgar pain?
The potter's wheel for thee, and some coarse clay!

"So work, if work thou must, O humbly skilled!
Thou hast not known the Master; in thy soul
His spirit moves not with a sweet control;
Thou art outside, and art not of the guild."

Thereat, I rose, and from his presence passed,
But, going, murmured: "To the God above,
Who holds my heart, and knows its store of love
I turn from thee, thou proud iconoclast."

Then on the shore God stooped to me, and said:
"He spake the truth: even so the springs are set
That move thy life, nor will they suffer let,
Nor change their scope; else, living, thou wert dead.

"This is thy life: indulge its natural flow,
And carve these forms. They yet may find a place
On shelves for them reserved. In any case,
I bid thee carve them, knowing what I know."

The narrator was attempting a task which, to discharge adequately, required qualities and skills which he did not yet possess. The voice of truth reminds him of this and also that there are others obligations to be discharged which are well within his scope. His ego however is the driving motive. He has not yet surrendered this to the Master, who might then be able to work through him. It is his own will, not God's will, which he is following. The fourth verse shows that he is not yet ready to face the truth: he lacks the humility which would permit him to be of the Guild (i.e., an initiated soul). When God speaks to him, it is not with any suggestion of discouragement. It is the Voice of infinite patience which knows that the rose cannot be made to open before its time, and that to try to force it open is useless. He is advised to continue with what he is doing: it will have its value – perhaps the not the least part will be to teach him something important about himself. The ego-activity is not necessarily worthless: indeed, the path of desire must be worked out before the path of Light (the surrendered life) can be lived.

The teachings which Krishna gives to Arjuna in the *Gita* about action and duty are the same as those given by all great Masters. In effect he says: everything that you want can be attained – if you want it enough. But you must be prepared to use the right means and pay the required price, which the law of karma will exact. Whole-hearted devotion to anything is really worship of that thing, and the result of worship is to be attached to that which is worshipped. In effect then, even high and noble desires can be pursued by the ego, but these will bring a soul back again into incarnation. Only the yearning for God (which is not a "desire") is beyond this risk. The *Gita* expresses the idea thus:

Many shining Beings and forms serve to lead men upward and help them to blossom in higher worlds; but blossoms fade, and the seed must fall once more into the Earth, for this Earth is the soil in which desires grow and have to be uprooted.

On the Path of Light, the initiated soul must yearn to reach only the Eternal: she must not allow herself to be enmeshed by the finite embodied forms, – the forms of creation. Such a one on this Path has to reverse a process which has been practised for hundreds of lives, viz., the desiring of finite things for one's self. All grasping at things in order to satisfy the personal self or ego, has to be surrendered. This is the constant battle of one walking on the Spiritual Path. There is no other way to God except through giving away all selfish desires – and this culminates in the giving away of the ego-self. All that then remains is the Supreme, for there is nothing now interposed between the soul and God. The key practice is of unselfish service in the spirit of Love, – and this rules no one out.

To those who are initiated by a Master and are climbing the Spiritual Path up the final Mountain, nothing can matter except doing one's duty as directed. This duty is likely to be closely linked with concern for the welfare of others. Success and failure as judged by the world, are not the pilgrim's concern. Because we have to live in a society in which relationships with others are inevitable and important, we can appreciate A. H. Clough's poem:

Say not the struggle nought availeth,
　The labour and the wounds are vain,
The enemy faints not, nor faileth,
　And as things have been they remain.

If hopes were dupes, fears may be liars;
　It may be in yon smoke concealed,
Your comrades chase e'en now the fliers,
　And, but for you, possess the field.

For while the tired waves, vainly breaking,
　Seem here no painful inch to gain,
Far back, through creeks and inlets making,
　Comes silent, flooding in, the main.

And not by eastern windows only,
　When daylight comes, comes in the light,
In front, the sun climbs slow, how slowly,
　But westward, look, the land is bright!

Arthur Hugh Clough was writing almost a century and a half
ago (1819–1861), in the days before two world wars had dis-
illusioned us about the nature of progress, and also before
there was any substantial interest in the western world of the
teachings of the great sages of the east. I like to think however,
that his last verse is prophetic, and that the growing light, when
it dispels the thick darkness of this planet of ours, will be seen
as clearly through western windows as through eastern ones.
Ramakrishna once said, "The true religious teachers of all
climes and ages are like lamps through which is revealed the
Light of the Spirit, flowing constantly from the One Source,
the Almighty Lord."

Ramakrishna had some relevant things to say about work
and duty:

You cannot get rid of work, because Nature will lead you
on to it. That being so, let all work be done as it ought to be
done. If work is done unattached, it will lead to God. To
work without any attachment is to work without the expectation of any reward, or fear of any punishment in this world
or the next. Work so done is a means to the End, and God is
the End. The end of life is to see God. Let me repeat, that the

means should not be confounded with the end, that the first stage on a road should not be taken for the goal. Do not regard work as the be-all and end-all of human existence. Pray for devotion to God. Suppose you were fortunate enough to see God. Then what would you pray for? Would you pray for dispensaries and hospitals, tanks and wells, roads and alms-houses? No, these are realities to us so long as we do not see God. But once brought face to face with the Divine Vision, we see them as they are, transitory things, no better than dreams. Then we would pray for more Light, more Knowledge in the highest sense, more Divine Love, the Love which lifts us from man to God, the Love that makes us realise that we are really sons of the Supreme Being, of Whom all that can be said is that He exists, that He is Knowledge itself in the highest sense, and that He is the eternal fountain of Love and Bliss.

Perhaps bliss is as yet too far beyond us — something that we may hope to realise when that Vision is granted, but happiness is surely within our grasp, if we fulfil our duty, thinking of the Father, and offering all its fruits to Him. Robert Louis Stevenson must have thought so, and his prayer is one that we may frequently feel speaks to our condition.

> If I have faltered more or less
> In my great task of happiness;
> If I have moved among my race
> And shown no glorious morning face;
> If beams from happy human eyes
> Have moved me not; if morning skies,
> Books, and my food, and summer rain
> Knocked on my sullen heart in vain:-
> Lord, Thy most pointed pleasure take
> And stab my spirit broad awake;
> Or, Lord, if too obdurate I,
> Choose Thou, before that spirit die,
> A piercing pain, a killing sin,
> And to my dead heart run them in!

18

Appreciating the Present

SHELLEY IN HIS WELL-KNOWN *Ode to a Skylark*, CONTRASTS the rather melancholy state of man with the joyful abandonment of the bird. He remarks:

> We look before and after,
> And pine for what is not.

The human mind is closely related to Time, probably to a wide interval of time, so that it can feel irked by the restriction of its physical state of association with a body. The physical brain is undoubtedly an organ of restriction so far as mind is concerned, so that in our waking state of consciousness we are hemmed in by that very small time – interval which we call the "present moment" or "Now". In higher states of consciousness this specious "present moment" is wider. In very high states of consciousness, the specious present may be of the order of years. Normally when awake, we compensate for our restriction to so small an interval of time, by re-awakening memories of the past or imagining what may happen in the future. As human beings, we are certainly time-conscious creatures. Is this looking before and after to be deprecated?

First, it might be recognised that memory has a necessary function in life. If we had no memory to recall, we should have no sense of identity. We should not know that we were the same person that we were yesterday, nor that anyone else was the same. We should have no sense of responsibility and no obligations. If we could not imaginatively fling our minds forward into the future, there would be no such things as hope, no place for trust, and as far as one can see, self-consciousness would have no meaning. We are as we are, and it would seem that these faculties represent, on our low incarnate level of being, a pale reflection of the quality of eternity to which the soul is related.

The sages, with one voice, exhort us to live in the "present". Doubtless this is for practical reasons. The commonest reason for wandering into past memories or imagining future possibilities is that the present moment may hold but little interest, or may even be an experience of considerable unhappiness. Wandering into the memory of the past, or into the possibilities of the future may then be a form of escape. It is scarcely to be expected that anyone in such a position will avoid these activities, but excessive indulgence in them will make for life in a phantasy-world and neglect of the opportunity which life is providing for us, for growth of character. We all long for happiness, and it may be a temptation to rest satisfied with the relative happiness of escape from an unpleasant situation. Our enduring happiness must depend upon the quality of character we have attained, the measure of our trust in God, and our willingness to face difficulty rather than run away from it. The happiness that lasts is a by-product of courageous effort and real trust, knowing that the Father will never ask us to carry a burden that is beyond our power. The great sages have always taught the importance of surrender of the ego-self to God. Ramana Maharshi taught his disciples that it was foolishness to imagine that each one alone carried the cares, burdens, and responsibilities of his life. He said to them, "The Lord of the Universe bears the whole burden. You only imagine that you do. You can hand over all your burdens to Him. Whatever you have to do, you will be made an instrument for doing it at the right time." I wonder how many people feel they are burdened beyond endurance, yet at the same time have neglected, or never exercised, the simple habit of prayer – the prayer of complete surrender first, and then of petition for guidance and direction.

> The troubled man turned head away;
>   Heedless he saw the river gliding,
> The reeds of sword-steel, and the grey
>   Reflected clouds fast-riding;
> He saw the foam, the water's colour,

The whirlpools dwindling as they ran,
A leaf, a fly, a spinning bubble –
    He did not see a troubled man.

For this, a moment in an age,
    He paid no price, and gave no thought;
He ceased his spirit's weary search
    And took that instant all he sought.

(Frank Kendon)

The reason was that he had for a moment forgotten himself, so that God could take over. The present moment, as we well know, is the one portion of Time in which we can give or receive, in which we can learn and act. The past and future are both outside our conscious viewpoint: the present alone is ours to use. We make a great mistake if we believe that we should always be filling it with action in the outer world. If we were willing to devote it more often to sitting in the Silence with a placid mind, we would find a thinning of the veils which obscure our consciousness of God. We should also want to offer a prayer of thanksgiving for the constant rain of blessings which we generally take for granted. All our unhappiness is because we are constantly living in the atmosphere which our ego is creating. Sometimes it is one of resentment: life is unfair and unjust to us! Sometimes it is self-pity; we are suffering more than we can bear! Sometimes it is depression: we are angry, but don't want to admit it! The more we dwell with our egos, the heavier and more intolerable life appears to be. The less we dwell with them, the more it is possible for divine strength to enter and lift us into His marvellous Light.

In a short and simple poem, W. H. Davies has reminded us of the joy which we may find in ordinary life, if we are open enough to the present moment.

A Great Time.
Sweet Chance, that led my steps abroad,
    Beyond the town, where wild flowers grow –
A rainbow and a cuckoo, Lord,
    How rich and great the times are now!
        Know, all ye sheep
        And cows, that keep

On staring that I stand so long
  In grass that's wet with heavy rain –
A rainbow and a cuckoo's song
  May never come together again;
    May never come
    This side the tomb.

Tagore, in one of his letters to his friend C. F. Andrews said to him, "Happiness we go on missing in life, because it is so simple."

If we truly appreciate the present, there will be no regrets as it flows into the past, nor are we likely to repeat seriously the common lament, "There is not enough time."

Those who make this complaint may be interested in a poem of George Herbert called *Time*. It has the quaintness of the early seventeenth century but it is quite relevant to our own period.

Meeting with Time, "Slack thing," said I,
"Thy scythe is dull; whet it, for shame."
"No marvel, sir," he did reply,
"If it at length deserves some blame;
    But where one man would have me grind it
    Twenty for one too sharp do find it."

The speaker is addressing Time, a little impatient with the slow pace of change, and suggesting a more rapid tempo. Father Time replies to him that for each one who would offer this petition there are twenty who would make the opposite request.

"Perhaps some such of old did pass,
Who above all things loved this life;
To whom thy scythe a hatchet was,
Which now is but a pruning-knife.
    Christ's coming hath made man thy debtor,
    Since by the cutting he grows better."

"And in his blessing thou art blest;
For where thou only wert before
An executioner at best,
Thou art a gard'ner now; and more,

> An usher to convey our souls
> Beyond the utmost stars and poles."

The speaker replies to Father Time that perhaps those who would like Times's pace to be slower had an earlier life cut short. Now, since man has the teaching of Christ to show him how to live, the sense of quickly passing time should be more a stimulus to endeavour than a discouragement. Time, like Siva of the Hindu trinity, is both a conserver and sustainer, as well as a destroyer.

> "And this is that makes life so long,
> While it detains us from our God;
> Ev'n pleasures here increase the wrong,
> And length of days lengthens the rod.
> > Who wants the place where God doth dwell,
> > Partakes already half of hell.
>
> "Of what strange length must that needs be
> Which ev'n eternity excludes!"
> Thus far Time heard me patiently;
> Then chafing said: "This man deludes;
> > What do I here before his door?
> > He doth not crave less time, but more."

These two verses are based upon the quaint seventeenth-century theology which contrasted incarnate life in time with discarnate life in eternity, and which moreover postulated that here in a body, man was separated from God, while in the heaven-world to which he passed at death he would find himself in God's presence. On these naïve assumptions, length of days on earth should scarcely be something eagerly sought after by the devout. Father *Time*, perhaps accepting the theological assumptions of that era, but with an almost modern psychological insight, suggests that though the speaker may consciously affirm his wish for a short life, he is really opting for a long one!

The soul that knows its own immortality and recalls its long journey through many lives far sunk in the depths of time, smiles at this naïve theology. It knows that it is a long journey back to its heavenly Home, and that whether particular lives are short or long is relatively unimportant. What is important is that we should accept this challenging truth before it is too late to benefit by it: that time is given to us to learn how to love divinely and to serve unselfishly.

19

On Suffering

AT THE END OF HIS POEM ENTITLED *The Signature of Pain*, ALAN
Porter has written the following lines:

> Every countenance
> That warms and lights the heart of the beholder
> Shows, clear and true, the signature of pain.

Along with these lines I should like to place the verses of a well-
known hymn written by Dr George Matheson, a Scottish divine,
who in his later years was a victim of blindness.

> O Love that wilt not let me go,
>   I rest my weary soul in Thee:
> I give Thee back the life I owe,
> That in Thine ocean depths its flow
>   May richer, fuller be.
>
> O Light that followest all my way,
>   I yield my flickering torch to Thee:
> My heart restores its borrowed ray,
> That in Thy sunshine's blaze its day
>   May brighter, fairer be.
>
> O Joy that seekest me through pain,
>   I cannot close my heart to Thee:
> I trace the rainbow through the rain
> And feel the promise is not vain,
>   That morn shall tearless be.

O Cross that liftest up my head,
   I dare not ask to fly from Thee;
I lay in dust life's glory dead,
And from the ground there blossoms red
   Life that shall endless be.

Suffering in one of its many forms – pain of the body, anguish
of the mind, or darkness of the soul (when not one ray of Light
may be seen), presents a problem to the mind, and an experience
of sadness and loneliness to the heart. It is possible to read
about millions of homeless and starving people in India, and
about tens of thousands who are victims of war in Vietnam, but
until we have ourselves suffered, these things do not penetrate
our being very deeply. In extreme suffering a person feels
alone. He feels cut off from the stream of life and energy, carrying a burden which no-one else can take over or share. This
experience stimulates different reactions. Some feel resentment,
some feel depression (which is often repressed anger), some are
oppressed by meaninglessness, some are given to self-pity.
After such experience, a person can no longer occupy the ivory
tower of detachment, indifference, or mere academic discussion.
Some ask questions such as, "What have I done to deserve this?"
But who is this "I"? Is it an isolated bead of "I-ness", or is it
an endless series of beads linked by a thread? Another common
question asked is, "Why does suffering fall upon innocent
people?" But who are we to talk of "innocence" when we know
nothing of the causal chains which link this life with previous
lives? It is true that some answers can be given in terms of
reincarnation and karma and man's state of ignorance. Yet,
when we have looked with some relief at these explanations,
there remains a mystery about suffering. This mystery seems to
be linked with the Divine Being, with the process of Creation,
and the "fall" into Time. The fall into Time led souls further
and further away from their true Home into the realms of the
mind where the Opposites create an atmosphere of tension.
Here, both joy and suffering are the soul's teachers, and each
teaches what the other must leave untaught. This realm, and its
precipitate into the physical world is one in which we are
oppressed by tragedy, until we are able to view life in the setting
of a far greater whole. In Tagore's *Letters to a Friend*, he says
some wise and profound things about suffering.

The barrier of self is *maya*. When it is dispelled, then we, in our suffering have tasted the draught of sorrow that wells up from the heart of creation, flowing out to be merged and transformed into the sea of endless joy.

When we do not see ourselves in the Infinite, when we imagine our sorrow to be our very own, then life becomes untrue, and its burden becomes heavy. I understand more and more the truth of Buddha's teaching, that the root of all our miseries is this self-consciousness [ego]. We have to realise the consciousness of the All before we can solve the mystery of pain and be free.

Our emancipation lies through the path of suffering. We must unlock the gate of joy by the key of pain. Our heart is like a fountain. So long as it is driven through the narrow channel of self [ego] it is full of fear and doubt and sorrow; for then it is dark and does not know its end. But when it comes out into the open, on the bosom of the All, it glistens in the light and sings in the joy of freedom.

In his own inimitable way, Tagore is telling us that until we completely break away from the tyranny of the ego-self, and are ruled by the soul-consciousness (the "bosom of the All"), we are bound to suffer, but the suffering is worth-while.

In another letter to Andrews, he makes these observations on Creation and the inevitability of suffering:

The infinite Being is not complete if He remains absolutely infinite. He must realise Himself through the finite: i.e., through creation. The impulse to realise comes through the fullness of Joy; but the process must be through pain. You cannot ask why it should be so – why the Infinite should attain truth by passing through finitude; why the joy should be the cause of the suffering in order to come back to Itself, – for it is so. And when our minds are illumined, we feel glad that it is so.

When we fix all our attention on that side of the Infinite where it is pain and death, where it is in the process of fulfilment, we are overwhelmed. But we must know that there is the positive side; that always there is a completeness along with the incomplete. Otherwise there would be no pity in us for the suffering; no love in us for the imperfect.

The profound mystery of suffering seems to be at this point: that the Eternal One has limited Himself, so that He can be found in the lowliest of His creation. He has therefore made Himself vulnerable to the same suffering as we endure on all levels. The supreme evidence of this is the incarnation of Himself as "Avatars". These have entered fully into the depths of suffering. Such great Ones, who are themselves without the burdens of karma, voluntarily take upon themselves a load of mankind's karma, and thus raise the whole level of mankind's possible spiritual attainment. We finite folk who feel at times oppressed by the tragedies of the world, must remember that through His immanence on every level, God shares these with us. This thought leaves one overwhelmed by what Divine Love is doing *for us*.

I do not know any hymn which better repays meditation upon it than George Matheson's. It breathes the very spirit of acceptance and surrender to the Will of God. The Love, the Light and the Joy are His attributes, yet they are our inheritance too, because He created us: and the Cross of matter, which symbolises suffering – shall we not share this too? There come back to memory some sentences which Rabindranath Tagore wrote to an English lady, who had, I imagine, written to him after reading *Gitanjali*.

This I know, that the moment my God has created me, He has made Himself mine. He is ever active in the unfolding of my being through the experiences of life, and in the enfolding of it with the various forces and beauties of the world. The very fact of my existence carries an eternal guarantee of love.

The last sentence in Tagore's letter is where Matheson begins his hymn. In this love of the Father is our eternal guarantee of security – and only in this. There is a soul-weariness which supervenes when the suffering of the world has been gazed upon for too long. It becomes hard for the individual to realise that behind all these dense clouds of the earth's darkness, the divine Sun is still shining. Matheson sees that to the soul this is still true, however dark is the earthly scene. In his poem he has made the complete surrender which is perfect wisdom. God is in charge of things – not us.

The greatest soul who has walked the planet entertained no illusions about human nature. He voluntarily suffered the worst that men could do to Him. He need not have done so: He had the power to avoid it if He had chosen to do so. St John relates that a deputation of Greeks came to ask His disciples if they could see Jesus. We may infer that they brought a suggestion that He might visit their own country and teach there. He chose to stay in Judaea where he knew that the enmity of the Jewish hierarchy, who saw their power threatened, would lead to his death. He made clear that it was His choice by saying of His life, "No man taketh it from Me: I lay it down of Myself.". Before Pilate, Jesus again made His position clear when He said, "You would have no power over Me unless it had been given you from above." By His accepting the worst physical suffering that evil men could inflict, and by carrying alone the unutterable sadness of being "let down" by those in whom He might have expected to find some loyalty and support because of their years together, He entered into the darkness of human suffering, to show us for all time how great God's Love is. His trust in the Father was complete. What is our trust like?

20

Serenity Through Love and Trust

HOW STORM-TOSSED WE ARE, – WITHIN AND WITHOUT! ST MARK gives an account of an episode involving Jesus and His disciples on the Sea of Galilee.

> And a great storm of wind arose, and the waves beat into the boat, so that the boat was already filling. But He was in the stern, asleep on the cushion. They awoke Him and said to Him, "Teacher, do you not care if we perish?" And He awoke and rebuked the wind, and said to the sea, "Peace! Be still!" And the wind ceased and there was a great calm. He said to them, "Why are you afraid? Have you no faith?" And they were filled with awe, and said to one another, "Who then is this, that even the wind and sea obey Him?"

The key words of the narrative are in His question, "Why are you afraid?" He is saying, by implication, "If you really trusted Me there would be nothing to fear." Their question to Him, "Master, do you not care if we perish?" was answered by His action. Then He put to them the counter-question, "Why are you afraid?" Let us put this to ourselves, and we should probably have had to answer in that situation: First, we are dominated by our senses. We see the stormy sea and the frail boat, and think death is final and tragic. Secondly, we are really not quite sure how great is the love of the Master for each soul. Thirdly, we do not completely trust this love as we know we should.

Yet, we are so dear to Him that the best and highest human love pales into nothingness beside His. He told us that the only things which God witholds from His children are things which might impair our progress towards Him. He sees what these are and we don't! Should we not then completely trust Love of this quality? Strong human love wants to give everything to the beloved. Would He want to do less? *How much more*.

The disciples had no idea how much He cared, or they would never have framed the question as they did, "Master, do you not care . . . ?" His consciousness was fully aware of the outer situation. This time He changed it in order to teach them a lesson, doubtless anticipating that when future tests came they would have learned that nothing need ever make them afraid. By His action He had shown that He had the power to intervene effectively, and that in every situation they had a right to expect that Divine help would be available *at the right time*. Of course they marvelled at this power. We would have done. When they understood Him more fully, they would discover that a greater miracle was being wrought within themselves. From being fearful, anxious, ordinary men, attaching an undue importance to the senses and the transition that men call death, they would conquer such fear, and later "be glad to be counted worthy to suffer for His Name".

One of the most impressive things about the Master was that His trust in God was absolute, so that no situation of any kind could make Him afraid. He commanded great power, but He never used this to serve any personal ends. He was vulnerable to pain and suffering, and also to sadness (on behalf of others), but He was constantly attuned to the Father's will, so that He saw that what was happening was in the long run for the soul's benefit.

Unconditional trust is for many people a difficult attainment. Trust is more than a firm belief that God can be relied upon – for this places the emphasis upon mind. Faith is the willingness to act upon such *belief*, and it is good. But Trust takes the heart as its guide and is prepared to act upon the heart's promptings alone. There is an Old Testament story which seems a perfect illustration of trust. Three heroic Jews had defied the edict of Nebuchadnezzar the Babylonian king, that everyone should worship a golden image which he had caused to be erected. As a result, these three men were thrown into a fiery furnace, and according to all Natural law, they should have met a painful and agonising death. Their words to the king before being cast into the furnace perfectly exemplify trust. They said, "We have no need to answer thee in this matter. Our God, Whom we serve, is able to deliver us from the burning fiery furnace; and He will deliver us out of thy hand, O king! *But if not*, be it known unto thee, O king, that we will not serve thy gods, nor worship the golden image which thou hast set up." The narrative relates how they were thrown into the furnace, and how their lives were miraculously preserved. The spiritually significant thing is not that their physical lives were preserved (doubtless by the use of psychic forces as in fire-walking), but that they completely trusted God, *not knowing whether it was God's will that they should lose their lives or keep them.*

In such a situation, or its modern equivalent, what would we do? Cromwell is said to have exhorted his soldiers to "Trust in God and keep your powder dry". The Arabs have a similar proverb, "Trust in Allah and tie the camel's leg." In the contemporary situation we might say, "Trust in God and take out a good insurance policy". This is not absolute or unconditional trust. It is a qualified trust, doubtless defensible by worldly standards, and for all ordinary purposes, but it is scarcely appropriate if it is God we are trusting in. Reflecting upon this attitude, we can see that we are already sure of what we want (and therefore what we deem best!) and we are expecting God to endorse that view! Should He be unwilling to do this, then we must be prepared to act! Do we really know what is best? We are prone to imagine so, but how far do we see? God sees that to which we are blind: perhaps a particular weakness which in life after life has proved our undoing, and should be eradicated. To do this may necessitate a certain type of experience, but we are blind to this. From our limited viewpoint we cannot know what is best for our soul's development. To the Father this alone is of importance.

There is a fine razor-edged path to be drawn at many critical points of life. If I am physically ill, yet fail to visit a good doctor who is available, on the grounds that God allowed this illness to come to me, and He can easily remove it if He wishes to do so, I am behaving foolishly. A basic attitude of trust is good and right, put perhaps I am not applying this attitude in the right way. God can work through the doctor, and an inactivity in which I expect God to do for me what I am able to do for myself does not seem to show trust at the right place. The doctor might be God's channel of healing for me: he will not be able to heal me unless it is God's will. Therefore I should consult him. Having done so, trust is an attitude of heart towards God that is unchanged whether the illness remains with me or a cure is effected. Trust is an inner attitude of acceptance, and not an outer attitude of inactivity.

There is an Eastern story of a Dervish who fell into a river and could not swim. A man on the river bank saw his plight and called out, "Shall I get someone to help you ashore?" "No" said the Dervish. "Then do you wish to drown?" said the man on the river bank. "No" said the Dervish. "Well, what then do you want?" "God's will be done. What have I to do with wishing?" the Dervish replied. It is obvious that this man's trust was strong, but his point of application of it was questionable. By his attitude he was ignoring the provision of a man on the river bank who could help him. His trust would have been properly applied not by declining to cooperate with the helper, but of acceptance of whatever resulted when he did. We do not live here as separate insolated units, but as members one of another. The world has before it the example of Jesus Who went about doing good, and said, "The Son can do nothing save what He sees the Father doing." We are expected to act, but leave the results to the wisdom of the Father, to Whom we offer all our actions and our service with our love. There is no peace and serenity amid the storms of life unless we are sure of His great Love and are ready to trust Him.

> As we fall o'erawed
> Upon our faces, and are lifted higher
> By his great gentleness, and carried nigher
> Than unredeemèd angles, till we stand
> Even in the hollow of His hand, –
> Nay more! we lean upon His breast –
> *There*, there we find a point of perfect rest
> And glorious safety. There we see
> His thoughts to us-ward, thoughts of peace
> That stoop to tenderest love; that still increase
> With increase of our need; that never change,
> That never fail or falter or forget.
> . . .
> For I am poor and needy, yet
> The Lord Himself, Jehovah, *thinketh upon me*!

(F. R. Havergal)

21

In Defence of Romanticism

In one of John Buchan's delightful stories, a character Sir Edward Leithen defines romance as "something in life which happens with an exquisite aptness and a splendid finality, as if Fate had suddenly turned artist, something which catches the breath because it is so wholly right." This description is perfect. It recognises three elements: "an exquisite aptness" which is something wholly appropriate and satisfying to the heart; "a splendid finality" in the creation of something incapable of improvement; and the "artistry of Fate" so that we are sensible of beauty in both the means and the end.

The Old Testament has many stories in which these "romantic" elements occur. Notable among them is that of Joseph, a shepherd-boy in the land of Canaan. The favourite of his old father Jacob, he incurred his brothers' jealousy, and they found an opportunity to get rid of him by selling him to caravan traders bound for Egypt. By them he was sold as a slave to a high-ranking official who was the captain of Pharaoh's guard. He grew up in this household to be a handsome and trusted man of considerable moral and spiritual integrity. In addition to organising ability he had a flair for dream interpretation. The opportunity to interpret Pharaoh's dreams was given to him, and he told Pharaoh of a severe world-wide famine that was coming after some years of plenty. Given authority to do so he organised great wheat-storages and became Governor of Egypt. Not only was Egypt saved from disaster but she became the granary of the world to which other nations sent their officials to try to buy wheat. Joseph's erstwhile brothers came from Canaan to Egypt for this purpose, – and here begins the romantic interest. While they, naturally enough, did not recognise this high officer of state as the young brother whom they had sold into slavery, he recognised them at once. The record gives a fascinating account of the ways Joseph tested them and their integrity – finally disclosing to them who he was. In the end he says to them, "As for you, you meant evil against me: but God meant it for good, to bring it about that many people should be kept alive as they are today." Jacob, the old patriarch, who had supposed his son Joseph had been killed many years ago, then came to Egypt to meet his famous son, and lived there for seventeen years on a property which Pharaoh provided. When, after Jacob's death, Joseph made a journey to Canaan to bury the patriarch's body "in the land of his fathers", there accompanied them to the North a great cavalcade of Egyptian chariots and horsemen. When the local Canaanites saw the spectacle, they said, "This is a grievous mourning to the Egyptians."

Equally romantic are many episodes in the life of Moses. One of the best known arises with the very beginning of his life. Owing to the growth of the Hebrew population Pharaoh had decreed that male children were to killed. The mother of Moses preserved his life by her courage and resourcefulness. Placing him in a waterproof basket in rushes near the favourite bathing-place of the Pharaoh's daughter, his mother stood not far away and watched events. The babe was found and admired; the mother offered her services to Pharaoh's daughter and was accepted. Thus Moses was brought up and educated under royal patronage and at the royal expense by his own mother. In this way he acquired an understanding of the Pharaoh and his outlook which served him well in the task of later years of liberating his people from their slavery. The "romantic" attitude to life contrasts with the logical and rational one. The unexpected and unpredictable steps in at the right time to create a situation which the heart feels is right.

The epithet "romantic" is frequently applied in English literature to a number of 19th century poets, Gray, Byron, Coleridge, Wordsworth, Shelley and Keats, whose voices were often raised in protest against the realism and harsh material-ism of their time. They felt deeply, and directed attention to the intuitions and aspirations of men's hearts. The beauty of Nature and the significance underlying the Natural order was a favourite theme. It may perhaps be illustrated by a lyric of William Watson which is markedly romantic in both its style and substance. Logically, all that this lyric contains could have been expressed in a sentence spoken by a man to the woman he loved, "I don't ask you for an immediate answer, but perhaps I can ask for it tonight?" The poem describes a setting which is exquisitely apt, artistically satisfying, and which from its appropriate timing will doubtless have a successful and splendid finality about it!

> Tell me not now, if love for love
> > Thou can'st return,
> Now, while around us and above
> > Day's flambeaux burn,
> Not in clear noon, with speech as clear,
> > Thy heart avow,
> For every gossip wind to hear:
> > Tell me not now!
>
> Tell me not now the tidings sweet,
> > The news divine;
> A little longer at thy feet
> > Leave me to pine.
> I would not have the gadding bird
> > Hear from his bough;
> Nay, though I famish for a word,
> > Tell me not now!
>
> But when deep trances of delight
> > All Nature seal,
> When round the world the arms of Night
> > Caressing steal,
> When rose to dreaming rose says "*Dear*",
> > "Dearest," – and when
> Heaven sighs her secret in Earth's ear,
> > Ah, tell me then!

One of the romantic concepts of mythology which some occult teachers seem to regard as embodying literal rather than symbolic truth, is that of the existence among human beings of "affinities" or "twin-souls". The suggestion is that the Creator, when he formed souls broke some of them into two halves and sent them, complementary and incomplete, on their long journey through Time. In the course of innumerable lives, caught on the wheel of births and deaths, they may occasionally meet. When they do so there is a powerful mutual attraction and the recognition of a perfect relationship. Separated again by the turning wheel, each is for ever seeking for its soul-mate. They must meet again in a perfected state of consciousness which transcends duality before the goal of the long journey closes. It is an interesting myth, probably pointing in the right direction, whether it contains literal truth or not. Between the sexes we can appreciate a polarity on many levels. Emotionally, we sometimes find the strong attraction of complementariness, in which one perfectly meets the needs of the other. On the level of mind we sometimes find the same perfect understanding, a rare thing, but not unknown. The Chinese tradition spoke of it as the "yang" and the "yin". Between human beings who love each other enough it is a longing to overcome the restricting barriers of personality and mystically know another soul. The broken duality of the myth may symbolise a longing for the wholeness of unity at some high level, and it is noteworthy that in high mystical experience this sense of Unity seems all-pervading.

The longing of two souls to transcend duality may be the first step towards an ever-widening transcendence in which "Groups of Souls" appreciate a special unity. Such Groups may have themselves powerful links with other Groups leading on to greater Wholes which journey together in Eternity. I have long felt that such a progressive unification at high levels of consciousness must point to Truth. It would indeed be a Unity in Diversity, and its sweep is from microcosm to macrocosm.

The deepest Truth must surely be that all our profoundest individual longing is for the One, – however fascinated we may be on these lowly levels by Its myriad facets. In other words, all our partial or "individual" loves are fragmentary reflections of the One Beloved Who is Infinite.

> I sometimes think that a mighty Lover
> Takes every burning kiss we give.
> His lights are those which round us hover:
> For Him alone our lives we live.

A. E., the Irish mystical poet who wrote this verse, saw the relativity of all these relationships in time, and knew that they pointed to the Eternal. God is the great and only Lover of man's soul: but how long man takes to make this discovery!

How shallow is the mere that dreams,
Its depth of blue is from the skies,
And from a distant sun the gleams
And lovely light within your eyes.

We deem our love so infinite
Because the god is everywhere,
And love awakening is made bright
And bathed in that diviner air.

We go on our enchanted way
And deem our hours immortal hours,
Who are but shadow kings that play
With mirrored majesties and powers.

22

The Soul's Yearning

A VERSE OF MUSIC BY VAUGHAN WILLIAMS* HAS BEEN ATTRACTIVELY
wedded to words of the fifteenth century by Bianco de Siena.
These were put into a modern idiom by R. F. Littledale, and are
quoted below. I would like to draw my reader's attention to this
hymn, if his mood is aspiring towards worship.

> Come down, O Love Divine,
> Seek Thou this soul of mine,
> And visit it with Thine own ardour glowing;
> O Comforter, draw near,
> Within my heart appear,
> And kindle it, Thy holy flame bestowing.
>
> O let it freely burn,
> Till earthly passions turn
> To dust and ashes, in its heat consuming;
> And let Thy glorious Light
> Shine ever on my sight,
> And clothe me round, the while my path illuming.
>
> Let holy charity
> Mine outward vesture be,
> And lowliness become mine inner clothing;
> True lowliness of heart,
> Which takes the humbler part,
> And o'er its own shortcomings weeps with loathing.

*The tune called *Down Ampney* by R. Vaughan Williams is found in the British
Methodist Hymnbook (No. 273).

And so the yearning strong,
With which the soul will long,
Shall far outpass the power of human telling;
For none can gues its grace
Till he becomes the place
Wherein the Holy Spirit makes His dwelling.

Another poet once said, "For Thou hast made us lonely that Thou mayest heal our loneliness with Thyself." The words of the hymn quoted are a prayer of the human soul to the Holy Spirit of God. Human love when it is pure and true, brings a glow of light and warmth to the Belovèd. Must not the divine Love of the Father, infinitely greater and purer, bring to the heart which It kindles and the soul which It visits an unspeakable Flame? In its radiant glow the Divine Love burns away all earthly passions and desires for persons or things. The poet prays that this glorious warmth and light may remain ever with him and irradiate the path of life which his feet are destined to tread.

The third verse speaks of the two orientations necessary to a pilgrim-soul who is seeking to walk the Spiritual Path. Outwardly she must be concerned with unstinted selfless service, inwardly she must be concerned with a humble and lowly heart. She prays contritely over her own shortcomings.

The fourth verse portrays the situation of every soul which for a moment has received the grace of visitation by Divine Love. Such Joy, Bliss, and Peace cannot be communicated, for there are no words to convey them. Even the poet's tongue and the musician's genius fail to express more than a hint of them. Only the soul which has welcomed this Divine Guest can know what this experience is. To have had one such moment in a lifetime is an unspeakable privilege. Its full impact may fade with memory, yet the recollection that such a moment was a reality will remain to bless the pilgrim.

To Enlightened souls who are conscious on all levels of Reality, and see every level filled with God, there is complete and perfect peace within, even when storms are raging round about. The mystic who falls back again from his high moment to the ordinary level of consciousness, has consciously to nourish his trust. The mind of man with all the lower levels, is ruled over by the Ego, and we know that this false self will fight to the very last for its existence. It whispers afterwards to the pilgrim-soul, "Can that high moment be trusted? How do you know that it was not delusion, – perhaps imagination a little over-stimulated?" The answer comes in meditation, when the mind is silent and the voice of the heart and soul may be heard. We are then reassured. That which is true is known to be true, and by trusting it we are not let down.

The Voice of the Soul says to every earnest seeker, "Trust, and walk on." No logical proof of the validity of spiritual experience is possible, but the heart has its reasons, and a life which is lived trusting in God discovers an unfailing certainty. Henry Bryan Binns expressed this in a poem:

I waited: He is come. Oh, I have dreamed
    Of Him and doubted; now, I understand –
In all the day it was His glory gleamed,
    In all the darkness I have touched His hand.

'Tis the new life beginning; now I see
    This cell is grown too small to hold me: I
Am driven out by joy's necessity,
    For if I were to linger, joy must die.

So I must out and on. Fling the door wide
    Good Porter, whether thou be life or death!
These narrow walls are not for me, outside
    The whole world breathes the wonder of His breath.

Does not this testimony ring a bell? We are born into this world, only to make this discovery, for by it alone are we lifted from the confinement and restriction of the body to live in the infinite realms of Divine Reality. No soul that has started its awakening from the sleep of the ages can ever again be content merely with its physical embodiment. "This cell is grown too small to hold me."

But here we are. We did not choose to come, and some of us were reluctant. After many hundreds of lives, the soul gets weary of the ever-turning wheel and seeks to be free. The body-brain ties it up to the present moment so that it cannot range over past or future. It restricts it also to a very small region of space. Beyond this, the mind restricts it to an almost impenetrable degree, – until God becomes real. The single viable cell within the acorn has no idea of its future life as an oak-tree, rising into the sun and air of the fields and skies. The ordinary human soul has not the faintest conception of what God-like freedom means. From time to time Enlightened Souls Who come to earth awaken other souls from the sleep of human life, and place their feet on the path to Freedom. How keen are we that this should happen to us? Can we shake off the lethargy, the habitual reactions, the attachments and comforts to which we cling – and the mental clothing that we have found so comfortable? Knowledge of God is the Pearl of Great Price, for which we must be ready to give away everything else, if need be. Are we ready to do this? It involves humility – "true lowliness of heart"; Love – "the holy flame" within; the selfless service or "holy charity" as the poet quaintly describes it.

John Masefield must have glimpsed the Pearl, for he once said:

The world is only a shadow of reality so beautiful that words cannot tell its beauty, so wise that words cannot convey its wisdom, so glorious that man can hardly bear to think of it. At certain moments of illumination the reality of the world becomes apparent, and its glory so magical that you have to cry aloud what you can of its wonder.

23

Beauty

HAVE WE EVER CONSIDERED WHAT SORT OF A WORLD IT WOULD BE if all that we call beautiful were removed from it? Suppose Nature presented us with no colours, or that the prevalent tints were dull greys, dirty browns or sickly yellows. Suppose Nature's handiwork was ugly or unshapely so that faces, for example, suggested a leer or a sense of frightfulness. Suppose all sound was noise and all scents were offensive to us, what should we think and feel about the world as a setting for human life? We mostly take for granted beauty that we have not created, and we often allow it to be despoiled.

All down the ages Beauty has been esteemed one of the three supreme Values of human life. Love (or Goodness), and Truth (or Wisdom), are the two others. All our intellectual analysis of them is talking around them. They are experienced from within as supreme Values. They are like the primary colours which, when perfectly blended make white light. As supreme Values, they must come from God revealing to us something of the Divine Spirit on all levels of creation.

Keats concluded one of his well-known poems with the words:

> "Beauty is Truth, Truth Beauty", that is all
> Ye know on earth, and all ye need to know.

I recall a statement made by the late Prof. Macneile Dixon, with which I feel a great deal of sympathy, to the effect that if ever he found himself in a paradise of surpassing beauty, he did not think he would be much troubled if the last secrets of the universe were withheld from him!

Here are a few wandering thoughts, speculations and intuitions about beauty.

(i) Most people suppose that we depend only upon our senses for the perception of beauty, but this cannot be so. The faculty which makes response to beauty lies far beyond the sensory level. Consider these strange facts about the senses. It is through the eyes that we appreciate colour, form and movement; it is through the ears that we appreciate music and rhythm; it is through touch that we appreciate texture, hot and cold, smooth and rough, etc; it is through the nose that we appreciate a wide variety of scents. Yet each of these organs when stimulated, only sends a stream of electrical impulses to a special part of the cerebral cortex. I have often asked myself – but have no explanation to offer – why different areas of the cortex, when stimulated, should offer us such varied sensations? Perhaps the cortex provides only a trigger – action to draw the attention of higher bodies to these happenings.

(ii) It has often been remarked that an event or place can be pleasant or unpleasant according to our mood, i.e., according to the inner contribution which we bring to the external stimulus. Such a statement as "All beauty lies in the beholder's eye" implies that the inner contribution is all-important. It is not the physical eye which is being referred to, but the subjective element. If, as suggested, the appreciation of beauty is a faculty of the higher Self, it may be that the external stimulus is but the primary fact in a chain-reaction which proceeds upward to the soul of man. The soul is derived from God. The more I reflect upon beauty, the more I see it as a form of God's grace.

Aeons ago, the souls of men left their native country, i.e., descended from the Divine Presence of their Creator. In His mercy they were allowed to carry with them some fading memories of the divine realms. These are the basis of our Values. When souls re-awaken these Values are reminders of that "imperial palace" whence we came. We are now responsible for the fact that we live on a diet of self-starvation for all the restrictions have been created by our ego-centred lower selves. They are not intrinsic to the level to which we have fallen. Whenever we respond for a moment to great Beauty we feel a kind of heart-ache because its essence is eluding us, and we know also that our experience is transient and Time will carry it away. In these high moments we do not want to talk : we want to worship.

Two verses of Longfellow's Legend of King Olaf are saying
something which is relevant here:

> As torrents in Summer
> Half-dried in their channels
> Suddenly rise though the
> Sky is still cloudless;
> (For rain has been falling
> Far off at their fountains):
>
> So hearts that are humble
> Fill full to o'erflowing;
> And they that behold it
> Marvel, – and know not
> That God at their fountains
> Far off has been raining.

It is the same affirmation which Krishna made when he said,
"I am Beauty Itself among beautiful things."

(iii) It is extraordinary to reflect how prolific is beauty, even
where there would normally be no human eye to notice it. For
thousands of millions of years there has existed an incredibly
vast universe, but only during the last three centuries has it been
disclosed by man's telescopes. Likewise there is a vast micro-
universe but it has only been disclosed recently through the
construction of microscopes.

It is only necessary to go down a thousand feet towards the
ocean-bed to find complete darkness, yet deep-sea fishes of the
most exquisite colourings are found there. As the poet Gray
wrote in his famous elegy:

> Full many a gem of purest ray serene
>   The dark unfathomed caves of ocean bear,
> Full many a flower is born to blush unseen
>   And waste its sweetness on the desert air.

When we consider the construction and colour of a peacock's
feather or a parrot's brilliant plumage, they suggest more the
Joy and ingenuity of an Artist than a means of sexual selection.
The grace of colour and form, and the ingenuity of construction
of many flowers likewise suggest more than the mere attraction

of insects involved in pollination. Looking at some aspects of
Nature's amazing creations, we may well ask by what prompting
and to what end is this beauty "in widest commonalty spread"?

I have found great pleasure in the verse of an Irish poet
Sydney Royse Lysaght. It is full of the sense of questing for
something that lies beyond the horizon of mind, or should we
simply say, "over the next hill". A.E. praised this quality of
Lysaght's poetry when he wrote,

> One mood is maintained almost through all the poems. He
> loves to dream of horizons, at what lies at the end of evening,
> a mood which almost everyone has, for it is the poetical mood
> most common to people who do not even read poetry . . . It
> is possible that many people have seen "the light that never
> was on sea or land" and had only a dull heart-ache at beauty
> which passed away from them, because they could not let
> down an anchor of words to hold the ship of dream.

Here is an example of Lysaght's poetry presenting the thought
that beauty is being created in places where no human eye is
ever likely to see it. The poem is called *A Silent Shore*.

> The solitude of shores by man unclaimed
> Peaks of unventured mountains, streams unnamed,
> And forests unexplored, and paths unknown,
> Lie here around us, still, and vast, and lone.
> No record of the years have they, no song,
> No tidings of unrest and right and wrong
> And hope and fear and love and death and birth,
> That weave the stormy story of the earth.
> But through the ages they have still pursued
> Primeval labours in their solitude;
> And through the silent centuries have won
> Secrets of beauty from the rain and sun;
> And from the morning mists and evening dew
> Fill up their treasuries of scent and hue.
>
> Here they have wrought a thousand years to dower
> With lovelier form the unbeholden flower,
> To hide the moonlight in a gem, or bring
> A subtler motion to an insect's wing,

Or to a bird's song add a note that tells
The joy that in their lonely labour dwells.
Here they have striven, age by age, to write
In things that perish, tidings infinite;
In things that change, the wonder that abides,
The hope that beckons and the love that hides.

(iv) All the arts are capable of conveying beauty. Walter Pater once made the interesting observation, "All the arts aspire to music." It is perhaps the most etherial of the arts: it can convey emotion strongly, it can inspire intuition, and it can point to things of the Spirit. Poetry as an art seems to lie somewhere between prose and music, for the former is naturally the vehicle of information or ideas and the latter of feeling. Thus it weds both heart and mind.

In a letter written towards the end of his life A.E. wrote, "I have tried in my poetry to make a record of moods which became transparencies into soul or spirit, and I have written no poetry without this idea." About a dozen years earlier he had written, "I have come to make one distinction, which is between ideas which are opaque, on whose loveliness we rest and are not carried beyond it, and ideas which are transparent and which open for us vistas, and start us on imaginary travels of our own."

I take as an illustration Alice Meynell's poem *The Visiting Sea* which possesses those qualities which I think A.E. would have described as "transparencies".

As the inhastening tide doth roll,
    Home from the deep, along the whole
Wide shining strand, and floods the caves,
    – Your love comes filling with happy waves
The open sea-shore of my soul.

But inland from the seaward spaces,
None knows, not even you, the places
    Brimmed at your coming, out of sight,
    – The little solitudes of delight
This tide constrains in dim embraces.

You see the happy shore, wave-rimmed,
But know not of the quiet dimmed
    Rivers your coming floods and fills,

The little pools 'mid happier hills,
My silent rivulets, over-brimmed.

What! I have secrets from you? Yes.
But, visiting Sea, your love doth press
   And reach in further than you know,
   And fills all these; and, when you go,
There's loneliness in loneliness.

In his book *Mysticism and Poetry*, Allen Brockington (a padre in the war), wrote these words:

I was watching a dying woman, and I noted in her face the ravages of disease. She was unconscious, and in her last moments of consciousness had said to me, "There must be no sense of hurry. There may be something to be seen or done, even now." I was standing at the foot of her bed, and I turned round and gazed at a portrait of her taken when she was a young woman. I could not help contrasting its clear beauty with the stricken face on the pillow.

Then I looked again, and the face on the pillow was infinitely – yes, infinitely the most beautiful I have seen. And I thought, "This is what she was meant to be. This is what she really is."

It was an intuition that completed all else: that in the life of men, their actual bodily life here, without disregarding anything that men call evil, there is a beauty inexpressible, and this inexpressible beauty is the truth of human existence.

24

Thoughts Facing Death

THERE CAN BE NO DOUBT THAT THE EGO FEARS EXTINCTION. IT IS probably the fear beyond all other fears in human nature. Since physical sense-data which have fed the ego through life vanish with death, this event on the surface *looks* like extinction. Human love then feels the sadness and grief of this event. What a poignant cry comes from the human heart in Tennyson's poem:

> Break, break, break,
>   On thy cold grey stones, O Sea!
> And I would that my tongue could utter
>   The thoughts that arise in me,
>
> O well for the fisherman's boy,
>   That he shouts with his sister at play!
> O well for the sailor lad,
>   That he sings in his boat on the bay!
>
> And the stately ships go on
>   To their haven under the hill;
> But O for the touch of a vanish'd hand
>   And the sound of a voice that is still.
>
> Break, break, break,
>   At the foot of thy crags O Sea!
> But the tender grace of a day that is dead
>   Will never come back to me.

The "haven under the hill" and the sea breaking at the foot of the cliffs remain for the eys of coming generations. Nature will continue its ceaseless rhythms as the centuries come and go, but the love and fellowship which gave meaning to the poet's life have gone for ever. He is expressing the age-old suffering of man facing the departure of someone who is beloved. I suppose that until man reaches Enlightenment and can experience simultaneously the relative unreality of the physical world and the greater reality of higher levels of consciousness, these emotions will remain poignant and strong.

At one period of my life, I weighed as objectively as I could the weight of evidence which bears upon the subject of man's survival of "death". Completely satisfying proof to the intellect is not easy to obtain because of the extra-sensory powers which minds have been shown to possess. Yet the very existence of these powers (which do not depend upon the physical brain) points strongly to the user of them as being essentially independent of his brain and body. These studies left me with the conviction, from which I have never swerved, that man's survival of death in the fullness of his powers is for practical purposes a certainty. It is a reliable assumption with which to live.

From a philosopher's viewpoint the existence of the *more* real cannot depend upon the *less* real in any essential sense. Mystics, who in higher states of consciousness have experienced the overwhelming Love of God, can never afterwards live as though ignorant of this Reality. This fact assures us of our eternal nature: *we are precious to Him*. Jesus once said to his hearers, "If ye, being evil, (i.e. imperfect) know how to give good gifts unto your children, how much more will your Heavenly Father give His Holy Spirit to them that ask Him." The idea that physical death could possibly be an end to what constitutes the true nature of a loving human being is fantastic. If the modern world were not so closely tied up with materialism through the senses, the idea would seem to be a prevalent anxiety neurosis. If we are rightly described in our essence as children of God, how *could* there be an end to our existence? To be loved by Him is the guarantee of our immortality.

To those who are certain that they have lived many times before this present life on earth, the issue of survival of death presents no doubt. What the soul has done many times before, it can presumably do again. In his poem *The Tragedy of Pompey the Great* John Masefield has the line, "Death opens unknown doors. It is most grand to die." This insight is surely endorsed by every mystic. Because of human nature, some grief will probably always remain linked with the transition of death. To this may be added feelings of unfulfilled tasks, of inadequate provision for others, and so forth. But who is wise enough to say what is incomplete, or who can assess from a higher standpoint what remains undone?

It is unjustifiably assumed by those who have not studied the evidence that no information of a reliable character as to the nature of life after death is available. On the contrary, there is an increasing number of modern books which offer evidence of high quality. I recorded in *The Light and the Gate* communications which I received through the script of the late Geraldine Cummins from my friend Ambrose Pratt, about nine years after his death. These scripts were quite authentic to me.* I may add that Miss Cummins was writing in London and knew nothing of my friendship with Ambrose Pratt in Melbourne. In 1965 Miss Jane Sherwood published a book called *Post-Mortem Journal* purporting to be communications from T. E. Lawrence of Arabia. For many reasons I consider this to be a genuine and valuable account of Lawrence's experiences. Of all the books which I have read, I specially recommend Helen Greaves' book *Testimony of Light*.† Miss Greaves' friend Frances Banks (between whom there had been a close relationship involving good telepathic rapport and much common spiritual aspiration on earth) took the initiative in communicating. The scripts which Miss Greaves received give a remarkable and convincing account of the work and progress of various souls who passed over. Love and selfless Service, together with Prayer and Meditation, are still the most important means of spiritual development there – as they are here. With the unfolding of ability to rise to higher levels of consciousness, Frances Banks became aware of her spiritual affinities where Groups of souls worked together with common aims and purposes. Such Groups of souls are probably closely related in sharing a common Unconscious Mind. On still higher levels of consciousness, vaster

---

* *The Light and the Gate*. Pp. 123–160. (Hodder & Stoughton Ltd).
† Published by Neville Spearman Ltd. Stocks of the book are held by The Churches' Fellowship for Psychical & Spiritual Studies, c/o St. Mary Abchurch, London, EC4N.7BA.

and more advanced Groups of Beings may link together smaller Soul-Groups such as we have described. The impression is that of a Hierarchy leading upwards to the highest levels of Spirit where there is a vastly expanded consciousness of Light. There is also an increasing sense of Unity and of the Divine Being or Divine Society.

On this physical level, while in physical bodies, we have only a restricted type of consciousness associated with the brain. This organ almost completely cuts us off from higher levels of consciousness. Truly, we can only see "through a glass darkly". Occasionally through meditation and divine grace we may glimpse the heights, but the clouds of our self-love and egotism come down one more and blot out the view.

How should we look at Life and Death? W. B. Yeats wrote an epitaph which was inscribed on his tombstone in 1939. This stands in the churchyard at Drumcliff, Co. Sligo, and it lies under the shadow of Ben Bulben (a mountain the poet loved). The epitaph reads:

"Cast a cold eye, on Life, on Death, Horseman pass by!"

He was no doubt affirming that life and death are illusions – phases of the ever-turning wheel of being. It is not on these that we should fasten our attention, but on the enduring character created through our experience of them.

In a famous elegy written to commemorate the death of his friend Keats, Shelley was able at last to write:

Peace, peace! he is not dead, he doth not sleep –
He hath awakened from the dream of life –
'Tis we, who lost in stormy visions, keep
With phantoms an unprofitable strife . . .

To those whose souls are awakening from the "dream of life" there can only be one purpose in coming again and again into a body, namely, to win our freedom from this cycle of necessity. To win this freedom involves the ability, while in a physical body, to rise above ordinary levels of consciousness to what is called full Illumination, or samadhi. If before the end of his earthly life, a man has not made some true progress towards this goal, the life and reincarnation may be considered a barren one, no matter what success the world ascribes to him. If a man has made true progress, he may greet the transition, like Mr Valiant-for-Truth, with confidence. In one of the finest passages in *The Pilgrim's Progress*, Bunyan makes his hero say, – When he has received the summons:

Then said he, I am going to my Father's; and though with great difficulty I have got hither, yet now I do not repent me of all the troubles I have been at to arrive where I am. My sword I give to him that shall succeed me in my pilgrimage, and my courage and skill to him that can get it. My marks and scars I carry with me, to be a witness for me that I have fought His battles, Who will now be my rewarder.

When the day that he must go hence was come, many accompanied him to the river-side, into which as he went, he said, "Death, where is thy sting?" And as he went down deeper he said, "Grave, where is thy victory?" So he passed over, and all the trumpets sounded for him on the other side.

25

"Not into Temptation"

THERE IS A PETITION IN THE LORD'S PRAYER WHICH READS, "LEAD us not into temptation". This has troubled many Christians who are puzzled by the suggestion that the Heavenly Father should lead anyone into temptation. If we suppose that Kal, the negative power, (or "Evil One") is responsible for all temptation, this would be consistent with the phrase in the prayer which follows it, "but deliver us from evil". The preposition "but" is probably the equivalent of "except Thou", so that the meaning of the two phrases would be "Bring us not into a situation of testing unless we are strong enough to emerge from the test victorious."

The testing of our qualities of character is surely necessary in life. How could courage be tested unless we were sometimes made to face fear or danger? How could fortitude and trust be tested unless we were faced with desperate situations which required us to "wait upon God"? The sense in which God leads us into situations of character-testing is surely the same as that in which seeds of karma are involved in the time-process. Karma rules all events, so that there are no accidents so far as human beings are concerned. All experiences into which we are led by the time-process, come to pass with the Father's approval. "Are not two sparrows sold for a farthing: yet not one of them falls to the ground without your Father knowing? Are you not of much more value than they?"

"Call the world," wrote Keats in one of his letters, "the vale of soul-making, then you will find out the use of the world."

Those who are familiar with the *Bhagavad Gita*, the most loved of Hindu scriptures, will recall that it opens with the scene of a battlefield. Two armies are drawn up in battle formation on the plane of Kurukshetra, and a civil war seems about to begin. Our sympathies are with Arjuna, a famous warrior, who is seated in his chariot a little ahead of the army of the Pandavas which he is leading. The five brothers (collectively called the Pandavas) are the rightful heirs to the kingdom. The kingdom has however been usurped by their cousins the Kauravas whose armies are drawn up defensively some distance away. Readers of the Gita know that its teachings are spiritual, so that everything described as though narrative, is symbolical. Kurukshetra is the battlefield of human life. Arjuna is a type of spiritually awakening soul. With him in his chariot (disguised however as a charioteer) is no less a person than the divine Krishna, an avatar or divine Incarnation. Krishna would be a figure whom we should regard as an embodiment of the Christ-consciousness. Arjuna is dejected as he looks around and sees relatives on both sides of the battlefield thirsting for the fight and prepared to kill each other for the sake of power and possessions. As a sensitive awakening soul, there is a deep conflict within him, and he is not sure where his duty lies, or even what is right. A desperately troubled man, he asks Krishna for guidance and advice. Interpreting the symbolism, the awakening soul Arjuna, has arrayed against him the army of his desires and beliefs, and friends which he formerly valued, and to which he still feels attachment. These are such things as worldly success, fame, security, traditions, customs and beliefs. These were expressions of things which were good in the past – at that earlier stage – but which have now served their purpose and must lie dead upon the battlefield of life if he is to make spiritual progress. Arjuna is inwardly asking himself whether victory on these terms is worth having. Is not the cost too great? If every other lovely pearl which he has collected must be given away to acquire the Pearl of Great Price, is it too much? What Arjuna does not realise at this stage of his growth is that having Krishna with him in his chariot, he has all that matters. The advice which Krishna gives to Arjuna has been discussed in § 17 *On Doing One's Duty*. We are here concerned with Arjuna's inner state – the testing to which he is being subjected. Perfecting character requires a considerable intensity of effort and many re-valuations. Look at some of these.

Duty. Tradition says, "You have responsibilities. You cannot just walk out and leave them to someone else." Jesus said to those whom He called, "Come, follow Me. Let the dead bury their dead."

Security. Tradition says, "You will find security in power, money, influence, and possessions." Jesus said, "Lay up for yourselves treasures in heaven ... for where your treasure is, there will your heart be also." God is your only security.

Sex. Tradition says, "Though often violently abused and degraded, if rightly controlled, this relationship can be a powerful bond between two people and is therefore to be cherished. Sages have taught that (except for purposes of procreation) it keeps those who indulge in it tied to lower rungs of the ladder of consciousness. Sex desire has therefore to be transcended on the Spiritual Path, where the mountain-top is the Goal.

Rights. Tradition says you have some worldly legal rights. Jesus said, "If you are struck on one cheek: you have another. Your citizenship is in Heaven."

Intellect. Tradition says that you must use your common sense and intellect wherever possible. The sages say "Recognise the limitations of intellect. Hand over all your problems to Him. Surrender completely to Him. Trust the Father and watch Him work."

Friends and Enemies. Tradition says, "Love your friends and hate your enemies." Jesus said, "Love is always right. Love your enemies too, and this will turn them into your friends."

Burdens. Tradition says, "You should carry your own burden, but it is good to help your neighbour." Sages say, "The advice is good provided your neighbour includes those who are not related to you as well as those who are. Watch that you do not help another to the point of 'cutting off his legs' i.e., to the point of making him dependent upon you."

For the person strongly attached to intellect, self-improvement may be the hardest task he can undertake. Intellect has been so highly esteemed by our western world, therefore the ego of such a one is generally strong. He has the hard task ahead of learning humility. It is difficult for him to break the habit of bringing every issue to the bar of reason and proof. From this habit he needs to pray for deliverance. Intellect is excellent as an instrument for unravelling the secrets of the physical world, but it is powerless to unravel the secrets of the higher mind, and hopeless in regard to the things of the Spirit.

I recall how my imagination was stimulated years ago by a statement of A. S. Eddington the Cambridge astronomer. He suggested that the number of stars in the universe might be comparable with the number of grains of sand on all the sea-shores of the world. I seldom walk along a sandy beach without this suggestion of Eddington coming to my mind. Then another thought arises: that the mind of man is inherently incapable of grasping these things.

> So runs my dream: but what am I?
> An infant crying in the night:
> An infant crying for the light:
> And with no language but a cry.

In spite of this limitation, Tennyson wrote sympathetically of his friend Hallam:

> Perplexed in faith, but pure in deeds,
> At last he beat his music out.
> There lives more faith in honest doubt,
> Believe me, than in half the creeds.
>
> He fought his doubts and gather'd strength;
> He would not make his judgment blind;
> He faced the spectres of the mind,
> And laid them: thus he came at length
>
> To find a stronger faith his own;
> And power was with him in the night,
> Which makes the darkness and the light,
> And dwells not in the light alone.

The person who longs for certainty about the things of the Spirit, has no option (at a certain point) but to set intellect aside, become truly humble and seek the mystical path which leads towards the heights of Truth. The mind has for many people seeking to approach the Mountain of God a duty to discharge. Near the mountain base its principal work has been done and trust in a Spiritual Guide becomes all-important.

I found him not in world or sun,
    Or eagle's wing or insect's eye;
    Nor through the questions men may try;
The petty cobwebs we have spun.

If e'er when faith had fallen asleep,
    I heard a voice, "Believe no more,"
    And heard an ever-breaking shore
That tumbled in the Godless deep;

A warmth within the breast would melt
    The freezing reason's colder part,
    And like a man in wrath the heart
Stood up and answer'd, "I have felt".

26

The Strangeness of Life

SOMETIMES THERE COMES INTO LIFE A PERIOD OF GREAT UNSETTLE-ment and much questioning. The foundations of the house in which we have lived for so long are shaking and rocking as though an earthquake is determined to destroy it, or at least show us whether we have built soundly enough. There may be different causes for this: the death of someone very close to us, a serious illness or accident, the departure to another country of someone who is loved, the destruction through fire or war or some natural disaster of the security which we have formerly taken for granted. When we have recovered from the first enormous shock, we start to reflect in our bewilderment on the "strangeness of life". We ask ourselves with new urgency the age-old questions. Is this life all, or can we look confidently to something better beyond it? Is there chance or accident in human affairs? Is the Pattern laid down and is our freedom an illusion? Most important question of all: Is there a Divine Love for us at the heart of existence?

With what philosophy the average man meets critical occasions, I do not know, but I imagine that time heals his wounds and the old outlook generally re-asserts itself. In a few cases the shock drives such a one to search desperately for God, or for some meaning in life. There is then only one thing to do: to go into the Silence and pray or meditate, so that the great Lover of our souls has a chance to speak through them and to them. One of the highest of all spiritual attainments is complete trust in God. How much or how little trust there is, can only be known when we face great danger or adversity. Trust in God is the inner equivalent of "flying blind" on a dark and stormy night in which the senses are of no help to us. If the Heavenly Father's great love for us cannot draw out our complete trust, then in what direction shall we turn? There is nowhere else to go.

Apart from the bewilderment of catastrophe, a surprising number of people have confessed that they have never felt quite at home in this world. I have felt this, particularly in recent years. Malcolm Muggeridge* has said that one of the first feelings in his early life was the overpowering one that "this world is not a place where I really belong".

William Watson wrote a short poem which he called "World-Strangeness". Its last verse runs:

> So, between the starry dome
>> And the floor of plains and seas,
> I have never felt at home,
>> Never wholly been at ease.

The Irish poet James Cousins wrote a poem which is a rather moving story of reflections of the pilgrim-soul in travail. The Voice is expressing the soul's longing for its freedom. The poem is in three parts:

> I am the voice of one who cries:
> Lo! I have lived my little day;
> Have looked within a woman's eyes,
> And seen them covered up with clay.

> And I have laughed as well as wept;
> Have found my foes, and made my friends.
> Through mighty issues I have slept –
> And waked to unmomentous ends:

> Have companied with hope and fear;
> Have followed Love's mysterious star,
> And dreamed it infinitely near –
> Yet found it infinitely far.

> And I have seen my fairy gold
> Turn all to dull misshapen lead;

*Malcolm Muggeridge, *Jesus Rediscovered*, p. 153 (Collins).

And hungry I have been, and cold,
And wished me harboured with the dead.

And sometimes I have longed to free
My soul from all that stains and mars,
To taste the quiet in the sea,
The peace that lodges with the stars.

The first four verses depict the tears, the tragedy, and the sense of disillusionment with incarnate life. The last verse expresses the soul's longing to break free. I have talked to many pilgrims on the Spiritual Path who are looking forward to "moving on". This world offers them nothing for which they crave, and their sense of exile and limitation here is keen. To use a phrase from the Epistle to the Hebrews, they feel "strangers and pilgrims on the earth". The second part of the poem continues:

I am the voice of one who cries:
Lo! I have stood beside the deep;
And I have watched the twilight skies
Grow grey with mystery and sleep,

While soft clouds held the last of light,
And furrowed all the sunset way
Where bent the silver scythe of night
To reap the aftermath of day.

And I have heard strange voices speak
In words half uttered, half withdrawn,
While far away a mountain peak
Put on the vestments of the dawn;

And o'er the adoring world there hung
Great silence as the Lord passed by,
And Day his golden censer swung
Across the altar of the sky.

No aspiring soul, however keen his sense of exile, has not at some time bowed in worship before the wonder, mystery and beauty of this world. The glorious forms and colours of sunset and dawn; the ripple of moonlight on the surface of some quiet lake; the majesty of mountain peaks; and the quaintly flowing music of mountain streams, remind every lover of Nature that

God is not apart from His world, but can be found hidden there as the very Spirit of it all – "Beauty Itself among beautiful things". The beauty is there for all to see, but men dwell in the shadows of their own creation and their eyes are blind to it. We miss the joy of the beautiful so often, because we are wrapped up in ourselves.

> I am the voice of one who cries:
> Lo! here I cannot stop or stay.
> I am not good, I am not wise,
> I only follow far away;
>
> And, seeing not, I yearn for sight
> To read the heart of praise or blame,
> To catch the beam within the light
> And feel the fire behind the flame;
>
> Or, rapt from all the tyrant hours
> That write their names in tears and blood,
> I long to pluck immortal flowers,
> And bathe me in a cool clear flood;
>
> And know that thing for which I seek
> With frustrate fingers blind and dead;
> And turn Truth's never-ceasing wheel,
> And from its distaff spin my thread.
>
> And so with ever-watching eyes
> I live my life from day to day.
> I am the voice of one who cries,
> And crying wander on my way.

This last group of verses express the soul's intense yearning to understand itself and its situation, – and to be understood. I sometimes pray the prayer, "Father, I do not understand myself; I do not understand anybody else; but I am so glad that by You, I am understood."

One recalls Tennyson's *In Memoriam* where, after trying to express his faith, the poet's last word is:

> Behold we know not anything;
> I can but trust that good shall fall
> At last – far off – at last, to all,
> And every winter change to spring.

So runs my dream: but what am I?
   An infant crying in the night:
   An infant crying for the light:
And with no language but a cry.

In our saddest hours we face the great mystery of Creation, Time, and human Life. We know that we cannot get far *with our minds*. We are indeed only "infants crying for the light, and with no language but a cry". The *heart* rises up however to make its response to the Divine love which bends over us as tenderly as a mother over a child. That Reality for which I seek is God. And when I find Him, has it not been promised that "God shall wipe away all tears from my eyes."?

27

On Judgment

IT IS STRANGE AND SAD THAT THE LANGUAGE OF LAW COURTS should ever have entered into Christian theology, for it contrasts so markedly with the language of the Spirit. It led to the fantastic conception of a 'Last Judgment', when presumably the successful would be separated from the failures, the redeemed from the condemned. What would be the fate of the latter is not made clear.

The concept of judgment in the sense of evaluating or estimating the soul's unfolding is one that we need, but the concept of God as a righteous Judge, with mankind arraigned in a court of justice is foreign to all that Jesus taught us of the nature of God. The poet who wrote of each man:

> . . . he ever bears about
> A silent court of justice in himself:
> Himself the judge and jury, and
> Himself the prisoner at the bar.

was far nearer to truth. "The Light which lighteth everyman coming into the world" (the Holy Spirit) is found in the soul of man. This divine Light is our constant and only judge, and It is perfect.

If anyone has been conditioned in childhood or youth to *fear* God rather than love and honour Him, let him read the most wonderful short story in the world, the parable of the Prodigal Son. The young man of this parable took his patrimony and wasted it in a far country. When through a severe famine he began to be in want, and hungry, he bethought himself of his father's home and began the long journey back. The Prodigal stands for the soul of every man, who aeons ago left the Creator's presence and journeyed forth to exercise his free will. He was a soul on the Path of Desire for many lives, but found himself without nourishment or sustenance. After suffering had left him desperate he resolved to return to his Father's home. The parable describes the Father as fully aware of the son's return journey, and says that at a certain point He ran to meet him. His welcome could not have been warmer, and the Father made no judgment of the son's conduct. He used no words that would add anything to his shame or suffering, but simply said to those around, "This, my son, was dead and is alive again; he was lost and is found." The great love of the Father had been unchanged through all the sad lost years and had finally brought him back home.

Surely this is the Divine Love, which calls for a response from us of love, not of fear. F. W. Faber wrote, more than a century ago:

> For the love of God is broader
> Than the measures of man's mind,
> And the heart of the Eternal
> Is most wonderfully kind.

"Kind" not "soft" is the word used, for the Father wants us back as sons not as servants. To return as sons we have to learn through suffering and joy, to taste the heights and depths of life and to choose Him because we love Him alone – and for His own sake. When we are judged by the Light within the soul, the all-important question asked of us is "How much have you loved?" We recall that Jesus spoke of this test in His parable of the sheep and the goats. He commended those who had given selfless love and service wherever they saw a need. "I was hungry and you gave me food; I was thirsty and you gave me drink; I was a stranger and you welcomed me; I was naked and you clothed me: I was sick and you visited me." We are judged by the love we have shown: no other criterion was of any significance in the parable. Is this too simple to be credible to the Church?

G. A. Studdert-Kennedy, a British padre during the First World War, wrote some verse under the stressful conditions of those blood-stained years. One of his poems he called *The Judge*:

> Methought it was the end of time,
>   The dawn of judgment day,
> The world stood waiting for the judge,
>   Dim faces drawn and grey.
>
> The sword of dawn's slashed through the East
>   I did not dare to see,
> And threw my arm across my face
>   From that dread mystery.
>
> Then trembling, raised reluctant eyes
>   To look upon the throne,
> But all the earth was emptiness,
>   And I stood all alone.
>
> Then I looked down, and at my feet,
>   With shining eyes and mild,
> And two small wounded hands held out,
>   There stood my judge – a child.

Studdert-Kennedy had seen the appalling suffering which war had brought to hundreds of thousands of children, and felt that by this alone it stood utterly condemned. (He was a pacifist.) But he is reminding us in the last verse of the nature of judgment itself – and of its costliness. The child-like spirit loves without any conditioning or limitations: that is its nature. To love unconditionally is to be very vulnerable to suffering, and even to be willing for ever to go on suffering. This is Christ's love, and it was the quality of this love which Jesus tried to convey to his not-too-sensitive disciples when He placed a child in the midst of them, and said, "Except ye become as little children, ye cannot enter the Kingdom of God."

This spirit exposes all our self-righteousness, our pride, our propensity to judge others, our fault-finding, our scepticism and our criticism. When we look within ourselves do we not find something of these besetting habits there? There is an old proverb which reads, "To know all would be to forgive all." Sometimes we come to know the sad story of a lost childhood: perhaps of the cruelty, unkindness, or indifference of adults who so behaved towards a child that he carries throughout adult life the indelible scars of not being loved for himself. Certainly if we could see all the factors, many of which reach back into former lives, which have operated to make a person what he is now, we should only feel more and more compassion and understanding. We should be driven to ask ourselves whether, in that situation we should have done any better, or even as well.

28

Dreams That Take the Breath Away

There is a poem by Charlotte Mew to which she gave
the simple title *In the Fields*:

> Lord, when I look at lovely things that pass,
>   Under old trees the shadows of young leaves
> Dancing to please the wind along the grass,
>   Or the gold stillness of the August sun on the August
>   sheaves;
> Can I believe there is a heavenlier world than this?
>   And if there is
> Will the strange heart of any everlasting thing
>   Bring me these dreams that take my breath away?
> They come at evening with the home-flying rooks and the
>   scent of hay
>   Over the fields. They come in Spring.

In the pattern of our industrial civilisation we have lost something very precious to the soul of man. It is much more accessible
amid the simplicity of country life, and many individuals pine
for it still. The congestion and artificiality of the world's great
cities condition individuals to accept this self-imposed horror.
Not many generations have passed since they knew seedtime
and harvest and were alive in contact with the good earth. Many
English poets have felt this nostalgia, and by their sensitivity
have kept us reminded of this other world and placed us deeply
in their debt. To read their verse helps us to slip away into an
older and truer setting of natural beauty and offer praise to
Him Who made it. The garment of Nature often calls forth

that essence of beauty which is stored within the ancient Self or Soul. Much of the poetry of A.E. makes reference to this power.

> I know when I come to my own Immortal, I will find
>   there
> In a myriad instant all that the wandering soul found
>   fair . . .

Perhaps this calling forth from the Soul is the essence of true imagination. Muriel Stuart went into a seed-shop and wrote:

> Here in a quiet and dusty room they lie,
> Faded as crumbled stone or shifting sand,
> Forlorn as ashes, shrivelled, scentless, dry –
> Meadows and gardens running through my hand.
>
> In this brown husk a dale of hawthorn dreams,
> A cedar in this narrow cell is thrust:
> It will drink deeply of a century's streams,
> These lilies shall make summer on my dust.
>
> Here in their safe and simple house of death,
> Sealed in their shells a million roses leap;
> Here I can blow a garden with my breath,
> And in my hand a forest lies asleep.

This delightful poem evokes the power of imagination, and sees hidden behind the outward husk of seed the mystery of life with its essence of beauty, colour and form. In Tennyson's phrase, the soul "hears the lark within the songless egg". In her poem Charlotte Mew asks the question, "Will the strange heart of any everlasting thing bring me these dreams that take my breath away?" The answer is surely "Yes", for that is where the essence of these dreams come from – higher levels of consciousness which are sometimes accessible to us. Everything beautiful that appears to us on the physical level is precipitated by the active imaginative power of great Beings who can operate on these higher levels. They are channels for the creative imagination of God.

I had a close friend, Ambrose Pratt, who passed over in

1944.* Nine years later, he made contact with me through the inspired writing of a well-known medium in London. In response to a question which I put to him about his special interests, he wrote through this medium, "I may say that I am training to become a seasonal organiser of bird-life in connection with the planet Earth. I am one of many souls who work at breath-of-life in regard to birds who are to be born each spring. The old patterns are conserved and there has to be a collective drive in regard to launching the young of each species every spring." This is apparently one of the many forms of artistic and creative activity which occupy souls on higher levels. Don't let us be content with the unthinking materialism which is satisfied to suppose that "things just happen". Familiarity can easily blind us to the wonder of the world.

On another occasion he wrote to me of a mystical type of experience. From his high level he had been viewing an island in the Gulf of Mexico. After studying it (or more probably, its etheric counterpart), his consciousness was lifted to a still higher level of which he wrote:

Then I knew the Unity behind the separate myriad forms animated by life on that small island. I was one with the Divine Imagining actively maintaining and conserving that fragment of Nature. I was one with the Artist experiencing the creative rapture that was His, one with the essence, the conception, and containing as well the physical representation ... I was aware of the large, the little, the infinitesimal, on that island. I experienced breath-of-life animating the tiniest coloured insect there; life in orange-grove, cedar, and tall waving palm; life in the black and white people on the island, and in animal existence there. But it came like a chorus, many voices making one earth-time song. I was aware of the whole, of each separately, and of activating creative bliss ... I saw the conception of each in the essence, so much more exquisite, finer, subtilised. The initiatory conception is a country where Beauty has no ebb, no decrease, no rotting or withering, where Joy is Wisdom, Time an endless melody. Mistakenly I use the verb "saw", but I experienced it within my whole being.

* I wrote of him in *The Light and the Gate*, p. 146–150 (Hodder & Stoughton Ltd).

This fascinating communication was attempting to convey how, from the great Artist-Creator's imagination, there flow forth a myriad "dreams that take the breath away". Here and there, a dream is captured by some sensitive prepared mind. If this is incarnate, the world will be enriched by some great discovery or invention, or work of art. Minds on higher levels, like that of my friend's, are apparently concerned with guiding the evolution of living creatures. The artistry of the world can have no known limits, and as our souls unfold their receptivity by growing more mature, we may expect to glimpse many more dreams "that take the breath away".

On the highest levels of Mind, with the Causal body as the only limiting vesture of the soul, we shall stand in the midst of finest dreams, for we are about to touch the outer garment of the Source, the fringe of the great Reality of Spirit. As the soul in its Causal body approaches the threshold of no-return is it prepared to discard this body and take the final leap into formlessness? On the Causal level we have the apotheosis of form where the finest of all creations are seeking their expression. The soul at this point is approaching the Gates of the Kingdom of God. All the wisdom, love and beauty that experience has gathered through innumerable lives in form will have been harvested in the soul, and the individual is subjected to its last testing – whatever this may be. Does it love and trust God so much that it can take the last leap from form into formlessness, from mortality into immortality as a Being of Light? All words and pictures fail us, for the created dreams give place to Reality, to the radiation of God Himself, where Space and Time are recognised as creations, and where there is infinite diversity within the Unity. The nature of this is all-Love.

Leaving the cosmic heights where imagination soars towards the Beatific Vision, we return to the level of earthly consciousness where we are living our little lives. Here men are caught on the ever-turning wheel of births and deaths, and for the most part seem unconcerned about their fate. Yet "dreams that take the breath away" are found on every level. We tend to label them mysteries and turn away, since familiarity has robbed us of any keen sense of their significance. Muriel Stuart's gifted imagination in a seed-shop lifts us up momentarily to view the wonder of life. Let us give thanks for all these glimpses.

The vision of one Man two thousand years ago still stands

unmatched. He chose to be born into a troubled country where Roman legions kept an uneasy peace, and where the professional custodians of religion observed laws and rituals, but practised very little love. The era was as unsettled and insecure as ours is today. The race appeared to be to the swift, and the battle to the strong (as the modern "nuclear club" bears witness). He gathered around Him a few men and women and taught them. His life was short, but full of love and compassion. He inspired some of them to view life in the same way. Then He made a deliberate choice: He allowed Himself to suffer a painful death at the hands of enemies who had long plotted to kill Him. He knew that victory would be His through suffering, and not by using the world's methods or weapons. "Be of good cheer," He said to His disciples, "I have overcome the world." It is a dream "that takes the breath away", and two thousand years have not dimmed its sublimity.

> Dear Christ, so long ago, so long ago,
> And men have dreamed again that gladness dies,
> Chanted her requiem and laid her low
> And turned to meet the smiling of her eyes.

29

God in Nature's Simplicity

ONE OF THE STATEMENTS MADE ABOUT MYSTICS IS THAT THEY have "a habit of mind which discerns the spiritual in common things". Eckhart, a great fourteenth-century mystic, once said, "The meanest thing that one knows in God, for instance, if one could understand a flower as it has its being in God, this would be a higher thing than the whole world". Blake wrote of "seeing a world in a grain of sand". Wordsworth wrote:

> To me, the meanest flower that blows, can give
> Thoughts that do often lie too deep for tears.

Henry Vaughan the seventeenth-century mystic, wrote, "Each bush and oak doth know I AM." Only a few days ago, a friend standing among trees and flowers in the garden, said, "How wonderful is all this, and how close to God one can feel in this setting." A mystic once said to me, "Every tree and living thing has its consciousness of God."

In a poem entitled *Reconciliation* A. E. wrote:

> I begin through the grass once again to be bound to the
> Lord:
>   I can see through a face that has faded, the face full of
> rest
> Of the earth, of the mother, my heart with her heart in
> accord,
>   As I lie 'mid the cool green tresses that mantle her
> breast
> I begin with the grass once again to be bound to the Lord.

Those who are familiar with this poet's outlook and intuitions will recall that he believed the physical world to be the body of a great planetary Spirit with which Nature mystics may commune. Such views would certainly not be regarded as incredible by students of astrology.

Henry van Dyke, in the romantic tradition of poetry, had a deep sensitivity to the simplicity of Nature's continuing life, activity which is so commonplace that we tend to take it for granted.

> These are the things I prize
> And hold of dearest worth:
> Light of the sapphire skies
> Peace of the silent hills,
> Shelter of forests, comfort of the grass,
> Music of birds, murmur of little rills,
> Shadow of clouds that swiftly pass,
> And after showers,
> The smell of flowers
> And of the good brown earth, –
> And best of all, along the way, friendship and mirth.
> So let me keep
> These treasures of the humble heart
> In true possession, owning them by love ...

In a little poem called *The Comforters*, Dora Sigerson speaks of the more-than-human comfort and sympathy which were offered to her by the raindrops, the sighing wind, and the grass over which she crouched down "dumb in despair".

> When I crept over the hill, broken with tears,
>   When I crouched down on the grass, dumb in despair,
> I heard the soft croon of the wind bend to my ears,
>   I felt the light kiss of the wind touching my hair.
>
> When I stood lone on the height my sorrow did speak,
>   As I went down the hill, I cried and I cried,
> The soft little hands of the rain stroking my cheek,
>   The kind little feet of the rain ran by my side.
>
> When I went to thy grave, broken with tears,
>   When I crouched down in the grass, dumb in despair,

I heard the sweet croon of the wind soft in my ears,
  I felt the kind lips of the wind touching my hair.

When I stood lone by the cross, sorrow did speak,
  When I went down the long hill, I cried and I cried,
The soft little hands of the rain stroked my pale cheek,
  The kind little feet of the rain ran by my side.

At a time of great sorrow the sensitive human being wants
to be silent and alone. He (or she) is passing through a
lonely and dark valley carrying a relationship from the lower
levels of the flesh, where it was familiar and precious, to the
uplands of the Spirit where once firmly planted it can never
wither. The rain and the wind and the moving grasses by the
wayside accentuate the loneliness of the journey, but they
are capable (as the poet found), of doing more than this.
They are saying to the traveller, "We understand: we too
pass away very soon. But don't be troubled or anxious. Rejoice that not a sparrow falls to the ground without the
Father's knowledge. He is all-Love, and He cares for the
least of us."

George Macdonald in *Somnium Mystici* tells how a snowdrop
lifted him into ecstasy so that "for one whole hour I praised
the God of snowdrops":

                    In the oval space
        A single snowdrop stood, a radiant bell
        Of silvery shine, stroked tenderly with rays
        Of delicate green that made the white appear
        As if the sun shone. With a faithful grace
        It bowed its head, as, in a world of fear,
        It could not be afraid. If it had swung
        Its pendent bell, and music silvery clear,
        Had with division sweet its sounds among,
        Dropped down its meaning tender as flakes of snow,
        It had not shed more influence as it rung,
        Than from its look along did gracious flow.
        I knew the flower; saw into its human ways;
        Beheld God's secret that had made it grow;
        And in my heart woke music's answering phrase.
        Nature's high laws, beauty's eternal birth,

And God Who bringeth life from out decays,
Light out of darkness, snowdrops from the earth –
Truth was all present in that little flower,
Instinct with the divine. A holy mirth
Awoke within my heart; for one whole hour
I praised the God of snowdrops. Then the stain
Of weariness fell. Gone was the sacred power
And gone the snowdrop from the window-pane.

The ways to God are infinite: they may start from the outside, but they all lead within, which is where the power lies by which a soul may tread them. MacDonald found one way through a snowdrop, but the starting-point may be anywhere. The mysticism of Francis Thompson frequently reminds us of this:

> When to the new eyes of thee
> All things by immortal power,
> Near or far,
> Hiddenly
> To each other linkèd are
> That thou canst not stir a flower
> Without troubling of a star ...

When this mystical insight has come, says the poet:

> seek no more
> O seek no more!
> Pass the hates of Luthany, tread the region Elenore.

The gates of Luthany are the entrance to the Spiritual Path, – a step which corresponds to Initiation by a Master. The region Elenore is the Path itself, – the hard ascent of the Mountain of God. In the parable of the Prodigal son Jesus called it the Way Home. Usually He referred to it as the Kingdom of God.

Western man, living in the great cities of our civilisation, seems to be fast approaching the point of complete enslavement to the machine he has created. Materialism and its values are thrust upon him from every direction. He has come to accept that his well-being has to do with science, economics, politics, and making money. The welfare of the soul is almost entirely neglected and his environment has a stranglehold upon him. It is an insidious situation from which most people in adult life would find it difficult to escape, even if they wanted to. Among the younger generation there is a naturally understandable rebellion. To what end is it all leading or serving? Happy are those whose destiny does not take them through the arid desert of this suffering. In a short poem called *The Choice* James Cousins speaks of "Life's deep desirings for the deep" which insistently call to us in times of meditation and silence.

> If choose I must a resting place
> What time my feet begin to fail,
> By God's most hospitable grace
> I choose a brookside in a vale.
>
> I ask not ocean's trumpetings
> Or hills that hearken to the skies,
> For one is loud with questionings,
> And one is quiet with replies.
>
> But by my brooklet's lyric leap
> My heart may contemplate at ease
> Life's deep desirings for the deep
> Mingled with mountain memories;
>
> And mine own rivulet of rhyme
> May run from summit unto sea,
> Singing between the banks of time
> The music of eternity.

30

Am I Awake?

ONE OF THE MANY STORIES TOLD ABOUT GAUTAMA THE BUDDHA is that awe-struck but curious listeners once said to him, "Who *are* you? Are you a god? Are you an angel? Are you a saint?" He shook his head and said to them "I am awake." The title *Buddha* means "The Awakened One" or the "Enlightened One", just as the title *Christ* means "the Anointed One".

I have been looking at a book by Arnold Bennett called *The Glimpse*. Half a century ago his novels of English provincial life had a considerable vogue and he became a "successful" man in the worldly sense. He was a man of the world. I mention these things because they make the more remarkable some of the things described in his book. He had a "glimpse", and here are some of the things he saw.

I saw myself in my moving prison, starved, nullified, unable to transmit to my envelope the perfected potential faculties which were within... I was constantly victimised by illusions and delusions ... the main idea underlying all its activity was wrong: the idea of gathering in instead of giving out. Its desires multiplied. Its imagined well-being depended on a daily increasing number of external things. That these multifarious things in no manner actually contributed to its well-being did not in the least discourage its obstinacy. The direction was diametrically wrong, and it hurried faster and faster in that direction...And worst, the persistent unwearied attempts towards self-aggrandisement of all kinds, towards the creation of a wall between the self and its fellows, towards the centralisation of the self upon itself, whereas the sole way of progress was so obviously in communion, in unifying, in the rich outpouring of self . . .

The strangest thing of all in that universe was not that I had accepted a mere harsh glitter as absolute beauty, nor that I had amused myself so childishly with vain toys, but that I had remained so long and co-completely in the conviction that bliss could alone proceed from the satisfaction of desire . . .

There are many profounder glimpses than this, and I shall quote one from R. H. Ward's book, *A Drug-Taker's Notes*.* The experience was unconnected with any artificial stimulus, and occurred as the narrator was walking home from the station. It appeared to be a going-up to a new level of consciousness and the writer says that he felt he must actually have looked different.

I could think-and-feel in a new way. When I thought-and-felt about someone with whom I had been travelling on the train a few minutes before, it was as if I recognised this person from a new angle. I understood him in a strangely objective way, which, while it was in no sense cold or uncaring, was quite detached. To put it in one way, I knew him much better, absent though he was, than I could ordinarily have done. And indeed, many things which I should ordinarily not have been detached about, presented themselves in the course of this walk as not mattering, – as being quite unimportant. But it was not exactly that they were trivial: they had simply got into their proper proportions . . . everything, whether things we attain in this life or miss, is (I now understood) acceptable and right. This, I realised was the real meaning of being "at peace with the world". But it was not at all the same thing as disregarding the world or being superior to it. It was accepting it. It was in a very new, but very real sense, loving it . . .

The writer describes how a familiar ugly little suburban villa, now appeared quite otherwise, and filled him with "indescribable joy".

* R. H. Ward, *A Drug-Taker's Notes* (Victor Gollancz Ltd).

After this, I began to look at everything around . . . everything I saw was mysterious and wonderful . . . The sheer joy I experienced in all this is beyond expression. I felt that the world of Nature was *utterly right* and literally an *act* of God's, and that to know this, and to be permitted to appreciate so much of the wonderful and adorable, was nothing less than bliss. *And this was reality.* That is the whole point. My knowledge of this reality *which lies beyond where we normally are* was undeniable and irrefutable. Nothing could shake my faith in it, either then, or now that the immediacy of the knowledge has passed . . .

The culminating experience was through an inner voice which said to him with unspeakable depths of meaning, "*There is something perfect.*"

It was a summary of what it is to be in the presence of God, Who is perfection's Self . . . and all the imperfections to which we are heirs could be seen in their insignificant proportions . . . I stood in the road filled to the brim with this wonderful and joyful realisation, that whatever we may have to endure of pain, sickness, grief, and man's inhumanity to man, *there is still something perfect in all created things, that ultimately they live by it, and that nothing else matters.* Tears fell from my eyes. I had an impulse to go on my knees, there in the road beneath the stars . . ."

[I have necessarily abbreviated this moving and remarkable account from Mr Ward's book.]

Every true mystic, indeed, every sensitive person walking on the Spiritual Path, knows that these are authentic glimpses of Truth. They are experiences of the world seen from higher levels. One might suppose that such experiences would only have to arrive to change the total orientation of the person and his attitude to life. Alas, this is seldom the case, and we are more like sleepers who awaken for a moment to clear consciousness and quickly lapse back into dream as the head touches the pillow again. How sad this is! Until a person is determined to keep awake to spiritual reality and to order his waking life accordingly, nothing can be done. It could have been the great opportunity of life – the immortal moment! We need to pray,

"Lord, help me to awaken, and never again be content to live this elusive dream of life according to the old pattern of values."

How can we waken up? When the soul has gone through enough suffering and comes into the presence of one who is already awake, this can happen. There are always great awakened souls walking the earth – in human bodies – who are prepared to lead back those who are ready to follow them to the Father's Home. Most men are not awake but are content to go on sleeping, or dreaming. Are we among these?

Many of us have read more than once, part of the narrative of the life of Jesus which reads (Matt 4: 18–22):

> As He walked by the Sea of Galilee He saw two brothers, Simon who is called Peter, and Andrew his brother, casting a net into the sea – for they were fishermen.
>
> And He said to them, "Follow Me, and I will make you fishers of men." Immediately they left their nets and followed Him.
>
> And going on from there He saw two other brothers, James the son of Zebedee, and John his brother . . . and He called them. Immediately they left the boat and their father, and followed Him.

It was a mark of insight and a miracle of decisiveness. If an Enlightened One called us, should we be able to make that kind of response?

Jesus is reported by St John to have said, "I am the Light of the World. He who follows after Me will not walk in darkness but will have the light of Life." Their own hearts, as they followed, must have told them of this truth.

Alice Meynell wrote:

> You never attained to Him? If to attain
> Be to abide, then that may be.
> Endless the way, followed with how much pain!
> The Way was He.

31

The Weakness of Persistent Incredulity

WHEN THINKING WITH THE MIND THE QUESTION IS "WHAT CAN I believe?" When reflecting in the heart, the question is, "In whom can I trust?"

St John's Gospel records that Jesus said to the listening crowd, "While you have the Light, believe in the Light, that you may become Sons of Light." The writer continues, "Though He (Jesus) had done so many signs before them, yet they did not believe in Him." The phrase "believe in" is clearly the equivalent of "trust". It refers to an orientation of the heart and soul and not to a conclusion of the mind.

Let us look briefly at this process of gathering knowledge with the mind, and where it had led us to. It has led to the widely practised outlook of materialism – to the popular attitude that the world the senses disclose is basic and real and the only one to be seriously reckoned with. Science, which looks so neat and tidy has abstracted from the totality of man's experience those elements which it could handle satisfactorily by its own techniques. It has "explained" these, and ignored the importance for the structure of the world of what does not fit into its formulae and theories. Here belong things that pertain to personality, emotions, creativity, aspirations, aesthetic sensitivity, moral sense and spiritual values. These are things which pertain to us as human beings. Intellectual knowledge which looks so completely tidy is knowledge acquired on one level only.

If we long for meanings in life we are compelled to use the heart as an instrument of understanding. The scientist – and most ordinary people – think that the drama of life is taking place outside them, in space and time. In a sense it is; but the sources and causes of the drama, and its modifications, are precipitated from inner and higher levels of ourselves. The art of living is manifesting from within us (where we are related to others); the outer world is but the stage of *effects* where the manifestation takes place in Time. In this sense the symphonies of Beethoven have been with us eternally, but the sensitive receptive nature of this man disclosed them to us. G. N. M. Tyrrell once said,

> The human being does not create the world in the sense of bringing anything actually into being, but he does so in the sense of acting as a selector of the aspects of reality to which he can respond and thus bringing these into existence for himself [and for others]. Instead of relying on the scrutiny of the physical world to provide us with a deeper insight into reality, we must look to the enlargement of the calibre of human personality ... The boundary which restricts our knowledge of the Real ... is in ourselves. It is a subjective boundary.

The person who is persistently incredulous of that to which his senses cannot respond should carefully consider this viewpoint.

I look upon mystics as the experimental scientists of the spiritual world. They have sought for first-hand evidence of God. Their method of seeking differs however from that of all other scientific questing. The natural scientist uses his senses and mind to observe and then interpret Nature. He may use elaborate instruments to assist him, but always as an observer, he stands apart from the data and forms his conclusions objectively. In contrast, the mystic is practising "the art of union with Reality". He longs to know God as an immediate experience. To approach this goal his soul has to be prepared, for he is both the observer and the instrument of knowledge. The way to such mystical knowledge or immediate experience is not easy. It involves great dedication, purification, many sacrifices and life-disciplines.

By religious organisations the mystic has usually been regarded as a thorn in the flesh. He speaks – if he speaks at all –

with the authority of first-hand knowledge. He is therefore a challenge and a danger to tradition.

The mystic has also been a puzzle to the materialistic camp, who say, in effect, "We cannot see what he sees!" This brings us round full circle to Tyrrell's dictum that "the boundary which restricts our knowledge of the Real is in ourselves. It is a subjective boundary."

If a man proposes to climb a Himalayan peak, he should certainly use his mind to plan the attempt, and draw on the experiences of others who have done similar climbing. Having done this, he should look for the best guide he can find, and then, roped to him, he must trust his guide.

The mind has its place in attempting to approach the mountain of God, but at a certain point near the base camp its principal work has been done. From then onwards, trust in the Guide becomes of paramount importance. I quote Tennyson's summing-up of his own position expressed in *The Ancient Sage*:

> If thou would'st hear the Nameless, and wilt dive
> Into the temple cave of thine own self,
> There, brooding by the central altar, thou
> May'st haply learn the Nameless hath a Voice,
> By which thou wilt abide if thou be wise,
> As if thou knowest tho' thou canst not know;
> For Knowledge is the swallow on the lake
> That sees and stirs the surface shadow there
> And never yet hath dipt into the abysm,
> The Abysm of all abysms, beneath, within,
> The blue of sky and sea, the green of earth . . .
>
> Thou can'st not prove the Nameless, O my son,
> Nor can'st thou prove the world thou movest in,
> Thou can'st not prove that thou art body alone,
> Nor can'st thou prove that thou art spirit alone,
> Nor can'st thou prove that thou art both in one:
> Thou can'st not prove thou art immortal, no
> Nor yet that thou art mortal – nay my son,
> Thou can'st not prove that I who speak with thee,
> Am not thyself in converse with thyself,
> For nothing worthy proving can be proven,
> Nor yet disproven: therefore thou be wise,

Cling ever to the sunnier side of doubt,
And cling to Faith beyond the forms of Faith.
She reels not in the storm of warring words,
She brightens at the clash of "Yes" and "No",
She sees the Best that glimmers through the Worst,
She feels the sun is hid but for a night,
She spies the summer through the winter bud,
She tastes the fruit before the blossom falls,
She hears the lark within the songless egg,
She finds the fountain where they wailed "Mirage".

32

The Poets and Bird Life

I DOUBT IF, AMONG THE CREATURES ON THE PLANET, ANY ASPECT OF God's creation has given to man more pure pleasure than bird life. Reading recently a book called *The Charm of Birds* by Grey of Fallodon, one realised afresh how varied and fascinating they are – in plumage and colour, in their migratory habits, in their mating and care of their young, in their nest-building habits, in their territorial attachments, and most of all in their song.

The English poets have for the most part been sensitive to the charm of birds, and scores of well-known poems celebrate their attractions. Among those chiefly favoured are the skylark, the nightingale, the thrush and the linnet, the magpie and the blackbird, the kingfisher and the cuckoo, waterfowl and seagull. Norman Gale in his poem *To a Lover of Birds* speaks of:

> God, Who gave the bird-folk song
> To draw the feet of Spring along
> The lovely avenues of birth . . .
> And dowered with heart and wing and voice
> The creatures that in softness match
> The lips of snow when kissing earth.

Of the birds most frequently celebrated in verse the skylark has pre-eminence, and tributes have been paid by Wordsworth, Shelley, Meredith, Bridges, Watson and many others. Wordsworth wrote:

> Etherial minstrel! Pilgrim of the sky!
> Dost thou despise the earth where cares abound?

Or while the wings aspire, are heart and eye
Both with thy nest upon the dewy ground?
Thy nest which thou canst drop into at will,
Those quivering wings composed, that music still.

To the last point of vision, and beyond
Mount, daring warbler! that love-prompted strain
– 'Twixt thee and thine a never-failing bond –
Thrills not the less the bosom of the plain:
Yet might'st thou seem, proud privilege! to sing
All independent of the leafy spring.

Leave to the nightingale her shady wood;
A privacy of glorious light is thine,
Whence thou dost pour upon the world a flood
Of harmony, with instinct more divine;
Type of the wise who soar, but never roam –
True to the kindred points of Heaven and Home!

Shelley's seventeen-verse poem begins:

Hail to thee, Blithe Spirit!
Bird thou never wert,
That from heaven, or near it
Pourest thy full heart
In profuse strains of unpremeditated art.

Grey makes an interesting comment: that in his youth he preferred Shelley's poem, but in later years Wordsworth's. The line of the latter which captivated him was: "A privacy of glorious light is thine." The rich and colourful similes of Shelley make it a more popular and better-known poem, but Wordsworth enters as an aspiring human soul into the symbolism of the lark's upward flight. Does it not portray the dual relationship of the soul, which as every mystic knows, must aspire Godward and at the same time, not lose touch with the everyday life of earth? One pole of the mystic's activity is the inner apiration of love towards the Divine, while the other pole is the selfless service of those who are with him on the ground. Has any finer description of meditation ever been given in verse, than that which attracted Grey: "A privacy of glorious light is thine."?

Meredith's poem *The Lark Ascending* begins well:

> He rises and begins to round
> He drops the silver chain of sound,
> Of many links without a break,
> In chirrup, whistle, slur and shake,
> All intervolved and spreading wide,
> Like water-dimples down a tide . . .

By its short lines, and the breathless absence of full-stops, it keeps us aware of the continuity of sound – "serenity in ravishment". Meredith seems to lack however the spiritual touch of Wordsworth, and also the appearance of spontaneous ecstasy which Shelley contrives to create. He is perhaps inclined to philosophise too self-consciously.

William Watson's poem *The First Skylark of Spring* effectively develops the theme of the contrasting conditions under which the poet and the bird are singing. The first three verses and the last two are given below:

> Two worlds hast thou to dwell in, Sweet, –
>   The virginal untroubled sky
> And this vext region at my feet, –
>   Alas, but one have I!
>
> To all my songs there clings the shade,
>   The dulling shade of mundane care.
> They amid mortal mists are made,
>   Thine in immortal air.
>
> My heart is dashed with griefs and fears;
>   My song comes fluttering and is gone.
> O high above the home of tears
>   Immortal Joy, sing on!
>
> For thou art native to the spheres,
>   And of the courts of heaven art free,
> And carriest to his temporal ears
>   News from eternity;
>
> And lead'st him to the dizzy verge,
>   And lur'st him o'er the dazzling line,
> Where mortal and immortal merge,
>   And human dies divine.

The nightingale is probably second only to the skylark in praise given to it by the poets. Keats' Ode is of course outstanding as romantic poetry. In the poem he is neither a spiritual teacher nor a moralist, but a sad, rather melancholy soul feeling "half in love with easeful death". He would like to escape from life:

> Where but to think is to be full of sorrow
> > And leaden-eyed despairs;
> Where Beauty cannot keep her lustrous eyes . . .

So, great poet as he is, he takes us "Through verdurous glooms and winding mossy ways", to the woodland haunts of this much envied bird. Here he can:

> in embalmèd darkness, guess each sweet
> Wherewith the seasonable month endows
> The grass, the thicket, and the fruit tree wild;
> > White hawthorn and the pastoral eglantine;
> > > Fast fading violets covered up in leaves;
> > > And mid-May's eldest child
> The coming musk-rose full of dewy wine,
> > The murmurous haunt of flies on summer eves."

The nightingale's song is expressing for the poet his own inner sadness in this "far country" of the world, especially as he reflects that the music he is listening to may be:

> Perhaps the self-same song that found a path
> > Through the sad heart of Ruth, when, sick for home,
> > She stood in tears amid the alien corn;
> > > The same that oft-times hath
> Charmed magic casements, opening on the foam
> Of perilous seas, in faery lands forlorn.

When Keats wafts his music through the air all the strings of the many – coloured land respond. We can linger with him and enjoy looking through the magic casements, but from time to time a cool breeze blows in from the hills of the Spirit – still to be climbed – reminding us not to linger too long.

It is tempting to look at other poets. Matthew Arnold in his poem *Philomela* summed up the nightingale's song as "Eternal passion! Eternal pain!"

Robert Bridges' poem *The Linnet* suggests that mankind with its sense of doubt, falls short of the bird's trust.

W. H. Davies in his short poem *The Kingfisher* uses this gaily-plumed bird with its preference for solitary places and green shady pools as a model for self-forgetfulness and humility. Thomas Hardy's poem, *The Darkling Thrush*, written about 1900, I always find rather moving. Night is falling on a grey countryside. The poet is standing there, a lonely figure, the light fading without, as the light of God has somewhat faded within. (His wife has left on record that as Hardy lay dying, his memory poignantly reverted to a deep early sorrow of the heart from which he never fully recovered.) As he stood by a gate, an aged thrush on a branch somewhere above, suddenly burst into an ecstasy of song, in such contrast with the dull environment that, says Hardy:

> . . . I could think there trembled through
>   His happy good-night air
> Some blessed Hope, whereof he knew
>   And I was unaware.

It is tempting to quote the poets who have written of seagulls, for their rather loud, plaintive, and even raucous calls as they glide overhead, bring back happy memories of my boyhood, of an old harbour on the Yorkshire coast, and of the smell of the sea. Instead, I shall conclude with six verses from a poem of W. C. Bryant, *To a Waterfowl*. The poet, conscious of the journey of human life, where often there are no paths and no guide-posts, takes courage from watching the steady flight of a bird against the sunset sky.

> Whither midst falling dew,
> While glow the heavens with the last steps of day,
> Far, through their rosy depths, dost thou pursue
>   Thy solitary way?
>   . . .
>   Seek'st thou the plashy brink
> Of weedy lake, or marge of river wide,
> Or where the rocking billows rise and sink
>   On the chafed ocean-side?

There is a Power whose care
Teaches thy way along that pathless coast –
The desert and illimitable air –
  Lone wandering, but not lost.

   . . .

And soon that toil shall end;
Soon shalt thou find a summer home and rest,
And scream among thy fellows; reeds shall bend
  Soon, o'er thy sheltered nest.

Thou'rt gone, the abyss of heaven
Hath swallowed up thy form; yet on my heart
Deeply has sunk the lesson thou hast given
  And shall not soon depart.

He who from zone to zone,
Guides through the boundless sky thy certain flight,
In the long way that I must tread alone,
  Will lead my steps aright.

33

Hymns to the Sea

UNLIKE NATURE'S VARIED PAGEANTRY ON LAND, THE SEA WHICH owes its colours largely to the sky, has been regarded as something untamed by man, and therefore to be feared. Yet, for countless centuries there have been men especially of the Northern races and coast-lines, who have had the sea "in their veins". They have felt at home on it, and earned their livelihood through it. They have both feared and loved it, while it has moulded their character.

It is not surprising to find that almost all the English poets have written of the sea. Perhaps this is because the variety of its aspects can match the variety of man's emotions. What the poet has to say about the sea usually reflects his own mood at the time.

If we look at the sea in a philosophical mood, we may picture our frail barques sailing over it as a parable of the voyage of human life.

> What mortal, when he saw,
> Life's voyage done, his heavenly Friend,
> Could ever yet dare tell Him fearlessly:
> "I have kept uninfringed my nature's law;
> The inly-written chart thou gavest me
> To guide me, I have steer'd by to the end"?

> (Matthew Arnold)

Or, in another reflective mood, we may feel the contrast between man's transient life on earth, and the enduring quality of the eternal sea. One may walk along a sandy beach, or watch the tide rolling in on some rocky coast, and reflect that in tens of thousands of years' time the sea will be doing the same thing. Those who live on the earth in far-distant ages will be able to watch the same panorama and hear the same sound of breakers on the open shore.

> It keeps eternal whisperings around
> Desolate shores, and with its mighty swell
> Gluts twice ten thousand cavers.

> (Keats)

Matthew Arnold, who frequently brought the sea into his verse, has given us exquisite lines such as "Murmurs and scents of the infinite sea". Equally however, he is responsible for some of the most melancholy lines. In his poem *Dover Beach* he describes:

> the grating roar
> Of pebbles which the waves suck back, and fling,
> At their return, up the high strand,
> Begin, and cease, and then again begin,
> With tremulous cadence slow, and bring
> The eternal note of sadness in.

His mind then travelled on to the decay of religious faith, (a phenomenon which seems to be mourned in every century):

> The sea of faith
> Was once, too, at the full, and round earth's shore
> Lay like the folds of a bright girdle furl'd;
> But now I only hear
> Its melancholy, long, withdrawing roar,
> Retreating to the breath
> Of the night-wind down the vast edges drear
> And naked shingles of the world.

In another mood, Matthew Arnold looks upon the sea as a separating and isolating force. In his poem entitled *To Marguerite* he writes of man's essential loneliness:

> Yes: in the sea of life enisl'd,
> With echoing straits between us thrown,
> Dotting the shoreless watery wild,
> We mortal millions live *alone*.

The poem is clearly alluding to some dear friend from whom he is parted, and with this thought obviously paramount he speaks of "the unplumb'd, salt, estranging sea".

Charles Mackay must have been looking at a grey wintry scene when he was led to write of

> the lonely margin of the sea
> Whose crested waves beat hoarsely on the shore
> Warring against it with perpetual feud.

In contrast with "the loud roarings of the tempest-waves", Shelley in another mood could write:

> down the steep path I wound
> To the sea-shore – the evening was most clear
> And beautiful, and there the sea I found
> Calm as a cradled child in dreamless slumber bound.

When the sea is in such a quiet mood, the sound it makes near the water's edge has fascinated the poets. Adelaide Procter writes of it as

> All still, all silent, save the sobbing rush
> Of rippling waves, that lapsed in silver hush
> upon the beach.

Shelley invites us to

> linger, where the pebble-paven shore,
> Under the quick, faint kisses of the sea,
> Trembles and sparkles as with ecstasy,
> Possessing and possessed by all that is
> Within that calm circumference of bliss.

The colours of the sea have perhaps had less than justice done to them. Jean Ingelow wrote that

the sea
Was filled with light; in clear blue caverns curled
The breakers, and they ran, and seemed to romp,
As playing at some rough and dangerous game,
While all the nearer waves rushed in to help,
And all the farther heaved their heads to peep,
And tossed the fishing boats.

Perhaps some poet will describe to us the fascinating pale green which lasts for so short a time as the "clear blue caverns" turn over into breakers.

The genius of Wordsworth, though nourished in the beauty of the English Lake District, can give us memorable verse no matter in what direction he turns it. I think the following lines, part of a sonnet, are quite outstanding among all sea-poetry:

It is a beauteous evening, calm and free;
The holy time is quiet as a Nun
Breathless with adoration; the broad sun
Is sinking down in its tranquillity;
The gentleness of heaven is on the Sea;
Listen! the mighty Being is awake,
And doth with his eternal motion make
A sound like thunder – everlastingly.

The poetic gifts of Alice Meynell (1847–1922) rise to their heights when human love is the central theme. In a poem entitled *The Visiting Sea*, the incoming tide flowing up a sandy shore is used as a simile of the love of a lover entering the heart of the beloved. It expresses delicacy, sensitive feeling and delight and is intermingled with the feminine mystique.

As the inhastening tide doth roll,
Home from the deep, along the whole
Long shining strand, and floods the caves,
Your love comes filling with happy waves
The open sea-shore of my soul.

But inland from the seaward spaces,
None knows, not even you, the places
Brimmed at your coming, out of sight

– The little solitudes of delight
This tide constrains in dim embraces.

You see the happy shore, wave-rimmed,
You know not of the quiet dimmed
Rivers your coming floods and fills,
The little pools 'mid happier hills,
By silent rivulets, over-brimmed.

What, I have secrets from you? Yes.
But visiting Sea, your love doth press
And reach in further than you know,
And fills all these; and, when you go,
There's loneliness in loneliness.

One aspect of the sea's activities has not so far been referred to. It inspired two exquisite lines of Keats, who wrote of

The moving waters at their priest-like task
Of pure ablution round earth's human shores.

Whether poets of the twenty-first century will find the same activity proceeding in days when great tankers are producing oil-slicks, and radio-active wastes are being thrown into its depths, is very doubtful. Man is a destructive creature, seldom willing to forgo immediate advantage for the sake of future good, until he is compelled to do so. One feels grateful that in spite of this, so much remains with us that is still beautiful. One calls to mind the re-assurance that, in spite of man, Beauty "immortal habitation has, though Beauty's form may fade and pass".

Does life offer a more exhilarating experience than a walk along a firm sandy beach at the beginning of a long summer day, sharing the resounding sea-music with others we love? What terms can express this timeless freedom? Perhaps it is a faint anticipation of experience on higher levels of consciousness where we merge with love and beauty, joy and freedom.

"Then I saw another angel flying in mid-heaven," writes St John, "with an eternal gospel to proclaim to those that dwell on earth, to every nation and tribe and tongue and people; and he said with a loud voice; 'Fear God, and give Him glory, for the hour of His judgment is come; and worship Him Who made heaven and earth, the sea, and the fountains of water'."

34

The Door in the Wall

THE SHORT STORIES OF MR H. G. WELLS WERE POPULAR READING in the earlier years of the century. Mr Wells was a fore-runner of the science-fiction story which has had a modern vogue, but he wrote many other stories which, while fascinating for their content, were symbolic of deeper truth. Of these, *The Door in the Wall* is perhaps my favourite. A brief summary follows.

The story is of a man who attained high position and success – but inwardly felt it was but dust and ashes – for he had missed something in life which had haunted him since childhood. As a child, he had once found his way (by chance?) through a green door in a white sunlit wall, and he entered a garden. It was no ordinary garden, but another world – colourful, beautiful and alluring, absolutely satisfying to his mind and heart. He had been compelled to leave it, and found himself once more, an ordinary little boy in an ordinary street, weeping bitterly. He had searched for the door many a time, but he had never been able to find it again. Later in his life, on six occasions, this very door had been presented to him at unexpected and inconvenient moments. On each occasion he had passed it by for what he regarded at the time as good and cogent reasons.

The first of these was in his schooldays. Some of the boys played a game which consisted of setting off from home ten minutes early, and making their way to school through unfamiliar streets, without being late. He was once playing this game when the green door in the white wall came into view. He dare not stay, for he was almost late, but he felt sure he would be able to find it again when he had time. Duty, discipline, and routine and social disapproval, were beginning to count with him.

The next occasion was when he was seventeen. He was in a taxi, going to catch a train to sit for an Oxford scholarship. He called out to the taxi-driver to stop, but suddenly realising how much hung upon the occasion – academic success, a career, etc., he countermanded the order. He caught the train, won a scholarship, and earned his father's rare praise.

The third occasion was one in which he imagined his honour was involved. There was an appointment to keep, and he knew that someone doubted if he would dare to come. He found the green door presented to him as he was hurrying past with no time to lose. Afterwards, he was extremely sorry. Years passed, and no sign of the door came to him again.

Later in life, the door appeared three times in one year. The first occasion was when he was hurrying to the House of Commons to vote in a critical division. The Government was saved by a majority of three. On the way in a car, he had passed the door: it was quite unmistakable in the moonlight.

The next occasion was one in which he was hurrying to see his father who was dying. The last occasion was when walking along with two influential political friends and the discussion was critical. He passed the door in the wall at arm's length, but to have turned aside then would have cost him a place in the new cabinet.

As he told this story of his life to his friend, his face was pale and drawn. He vowed that if ever the chance was offered to him again, he would enter that door and never return to what the world counted success – "a dry glitter of vanity".

His body was found a few days later at the bottom of an excavation which had been shut off from the street by hoardings, but a little green door which should have been locked, was ajar. Had an hallucination misled him? Had his haunting vision of the door betrayed him?

Mr Wells concludes by saying, "There you touch the inmost mystery of these dreamers, these men of vision . . . By our standards he walked out of security into darkness, danger, and death. But did he see like that?"

Mr Wells' story, of which only a brief summary has been given, is clearly an allegory of human life. A door appears to us perhaps on several occasions in our life. It may happen at any time: but we have freedom to enter or pass by. It is a spiritual door into an inner sanctuary: it is a precious centre of ourselves where love and peace reign. It is hidden within our earthly life, yet its bliss and peace are unearthly and divine. Wordsworth knew something about it, for he wrote, "Heaven lies about us in our infancy". To quote him further:

> Earth fills her lap with pleasures of her own;
> Yearnings she hath in her own natural kind,
> And even with something of a mother's mind
>   And no unworthy aim,
>   The homely nurse doth all she can
> To make her foster-child, her inmate, Man,
>   Forget the glories he hath known,
> And that imperial palace whence he came.

Man can never quite relinquish the search for something which his soul has known and which would mean the fulfilment of the deepest longings that he has. Yet no amount of intellectual seeking will offer him entry. The opportunity may be presented to him at intervals, but he can never command these occasions. The possibility of entry appears to be conditioned wholly by a willingness to put the door first, brooking no excuses, and considering everything else worthless compared to this. The same issue is presented by Jesus in the parable of the seeker for pearls. This man, having seen a Pearl of Great Price, is prepared to part with all the others to obtain this one. Notice in the story that on the half-dozen occasions when the opportunity was presented to him, he was not prepared to put its claims first. The alternatives were not in themselves unworthy or discreditable. A good logical case could be made for each of them.

In boyhood, it was easy to run past the door for there was still plenty of time to find it. All life lay ahead. His second chance, on the way to sit for a scholarship, symbolised the attraction of success, and all that ambition and enlightened self-interest could represent. On the third occasion his emotions were involved, but he was concerned also with what others would think of him. On the occasion of his hurrying to the House of Commons he could plead a paramount sense of duty to others and of public responsibilities which he had accepted. He could not let his side down. On the next occasion he was hurrying to say goodbye to his dying father. (On a similar occasion Jesus said, "Let the dead bury their dead".) On the last occasion reputation and the lure of high position held him bound.

How easily we delude ourselves! We say we have no time, but we have all the time there is. At every stage of life we can make good excuses for ourselves, but as the soul reflects afterwards on the choice it made, it is left sorrowful. We want security and we want Truth; we want worldly success and we want spiritual understanding; we want power and we also want peace; and we are compelled to choose in life between one good and a greater good. We think we can have both. I wonder if any good thing ever comes to us except in so far as we are prepared to sacrifice something which is in fact a lesser good? The supreme good, which is knowing God, demands from us all that we have and haunts us all the days of our many lives.

What do we say? We say, "The next time the door is presented, I will certainly enter." But when the time comes we find plausible reasons for our failure to do this. "I have a family that takes up all my time." "I cannot find a quiet place to meditate." "I have responsibilities to clients that it is my duty to discharge." "My wife (or husband) has a right to some of my company." "If I do not keep a close eye on the management, my business will break down," etc. The good is the enemy of the better, and the better of the best.

Wells' allegory suggests another thought. The door was presented in many different places and at very varied times. The spiritual door is in our midst all the time, but we cannot find the way in by cleverness or intellect. We are called when we are ready in soul. Our concern should be with self-surrender – an inner orientation which is best described as complete dedication, so that when these moments come we have prepared ourselves to take them.

In the allegory, Mr Wells leaves open the question whether through his physical death, the narrator had found what he was looking for. It is of no value to speculate upon this, for we do not know what point the soul had reached in its questing.

There is one practical question at which it is worth looking. What is the real importance of earth-life? In a sense this has been the underlying question in all these meditations. I recently read a book purporting to be communications from T. E. Lawrence* through Jane Sherwood. An interesting answer is given to the underlying question just mentioned.

There is a reason for stressing the importance of earth-experience. It seems that in the cycle of growth, this is the formative stage when any real growth in essence takes place. When the earth-life is over and one comes here, the law of affinity takes one into congenial conditions, and the general alleviation of circumstances removes all outer sources of conflict. There is no more struggle for existence. Our work here is a kind of mopping-up operation. We can, in fact we must, graduate from regions where our faults of temper and our sense of guilt are tolerated, to those regions where we have to clear ourselves of the stains of earth. But although we may clear ourselves, and in the ascent of the planes gradually purify our being until we are again essential spirit, still no actual growth in this spirit will have been made here. What we bring from earth remains our all, so our fate is bound up with our earth-experiences; only in the struggle and turmoil of life there, are we able to make any real difference to our spiritual stature. So, although this in-between period is a wonderful interlude, the real work has to be done on earth.

Nowhere else have I seen expressed so clearly the recognition that it is here on earth that our "spiritual capital" is built and augmented. It is not increased by our activities on higher planes of being after death. It is only purified, as it were, from the false coinage and false values which have been intermingled with it, and have no lasting contribution to make to the spiritual stature of the individual. If we accept this truth and build it into our outlook while here in a physical body, it should be an encouragement to face with courage whatever life is bringing to

* Jane Sherwood, *Post Mortem Journal* (Neville Spearman, London 1964). This interesting book rings true. I accept the authorship claimed.

us. That which we call character is grown under these conditions of the stress and storm of life. This can never be lost.

Oliver Wendell Holmes wrote a poem called *The Chambered Nautilus* and some lines from it may appropriately close this meditation.

Year after year beheld the silent toil
  That spread his lustrous coil;
  Still, as the spiral grew,
He left the past year's dwelling for the new,
Stole with soft step its shining archway through,
  Built up its idle door,
Stretched in his last-found home, and knew the old
no more.

      . . .

Build thee more stately mansions, O my soul,
' As the swift seasons roll!
  Leave thy low-vaulted past!
Let each new temple nobler than the last,
Shut thee from heaven with a dome more vast,
  Till thou at length art free,
leaving thine outgrown shell by life's unresting sea.

35

A Great Soul's Au Revoir

FOR THREE YEARS HE HAD WALKED THE HIGH-WAYS AND BY-WAYS of Palestine and the mission He had come to discharge was now approaching its climactic end. To one viewing the situation in terms of human reason, the end might with advantage have been delayed, but Divine Wisdom ordained otherwise. Jesus said to His disciples, "I will no longer talk much with you, for the ruler of this world is coming." (This means that the pre-ordained time for Kal, the negative power, to be in the ascendant, was fast coming.) "He has no power over Me; but I do as the Father has commanded Me, so that the world may know that I love the Father."

"The cross signifies," says Radhakrishnan, "that progress is achieved, not by those who fight for it, but by those who suffer for it."

The celebration of the Jewish passover made an adequate cover for the Last Supper. It was clearly planned ahead. It was the last opportunity He would have to share a meal with them, to strengthen the unique fellowship of the past three years, and to reinforce in them the timeless and eternal teachings. It was His poignant and intimate "au revoir". Luke specifically records the first words of His talk to them: "I have earnestly desired to eat this passover with you before I suffer . . ." It is perfectly clear that He knew what was going on in all their minds, and also in the minds of those who were plotting to destroy Him. The mind of Judas was an open book to Him, and He allowed the other disciples to know this at the right time. It is strange that, according to the records, not one of the eleven suspected Judas. Was Judas a "lone wolf" who kept his counsel? Did none of the others know him well enough even to suspect latent treachery? The attempt to excuse the conduct of Judas as an attempt to force His Master's hand into action, believing that He would then be compelled to take complete control, is difficult to reconcile with the despicable acceptance of thirty pieces of silver. With what sadness Jesus must have known this.

He also knew Peter's mind and foresaw his triple failure before the cock should crow the following morning. Peter had said in the presence of others, "Lord, I am willing to go with you to prison and to death." Even the prophetic warning was not enough. It is not so much Peter who stands under judgment; it is the weak self-centred ego-nature that is found in us all, and can never be trusted. It will deny even the Christ. The eleven were horrified at the mention of treachery, but even this disclosure made by Jesus did not alert them to the recognition that it was no ordinary passover meal which they were eating – but the last hour before the forces of evil struck at them. Jesus tried to tell them this: that the last three years were past, and the meal which they were now eating together marked the end of that phase.

Luke records that He said to them, "When I sent you out with no purse or bag or sandals, did you lack anything?" They said "Nothing". He said to them, "But now, let him who has a purse take it, and likewise a bag. And let him who has no sword sell his mantle and buy one." And they said, "Look, Lord, here are two swords." And He said to them, "It is enough".

He was trying to tell them in metaphor of the complete change that was coming and they could not understand. Perhaps they were all so wrapped up in themselves and their petty ego-concerns that they had no awareness of the great events about to happen? It appears that they had been recently disputing among themselves which of them was to be regarded as the greatest! Jesus had to remind them, "Let the greatest among you become as the youngest, and the leader as one who serves . . . I am among you as one who serves."

Two or three hours later in the garden of Gethsemane, the forces of evil were unleashed. Jesus knew that He had two or three hours before they came to arrest Him, and He spent the time in the Garden in an agony of prayer. Surely at no period of His life, in which He had utterly trusted the Heavenly Father, would silent human companionship have meant more to Him. In this very dark hour, not one of the three most trusted disciples kept awake, — even to pray. Could any loneliness have been greater? When He was led away, Mark says, in a sentence which surely plumbs the depths of human dereliction, "They all forsook Him and fled." This must have been the hardest thing of all to bear. These men had walked in the presence of His Light and all-Compassionate Love for three years. It was not their failure to be aware of the course of events, that really mattered: it was their failure in Love. He did not condemn them but He must have been very disappointed. Do not let *us* condemn: it is our *human nature* which is weak and untrustworthy, — as was theirs. It remains so until we are Illumined souls.

I find it difficult to believe that this great Enlightened One said on the Cross, — "My God, my God, why hast Thou forsaken Me?" How absurd to suppose that He started to think for the first time of Himself! What He probably said was "My God, my God, do not Thou forsake them." His loving thoughts would be with them so long as life remained in His body. These were the poor human channels through which the Living Water would have to flow if His work was to continue; these were the broken human lamps through which the Divine Light would have to shine on the world, now that He was going.

At the Supper Table, in this momentous hour, what things did he choose to say? Which of all the teachings did He represent to them for remembrance? The gospel of St John, written possibly seventy to a hundred years later, is probably our best guide, for it is a mystically inspired writing.
(1) He taught them the importance of humility by an acted parable. "Jesus, knowing that the Father had given all things into His hands, and that He had come from God and was going to God . . . began to wash the disciples' feet." It was more however than a lesson in humility, for, as a symbolic act, (as Jesus reminded Peter) He said, "If I do not wash you, you have no part in Me."
(2) Purification from all the dross of self-hood is essential to the Spiritual Path. It is the lower self (symbolised by the feet) that needs the cleansing. These are the physical and emotional natures and the lower mind.

(3) Jesus reminded them of the supreme importance of Love. "A new commandment I give unto you that you love one another; even as I have loved you that you also love one another. By this all men will know that you are my disciples, if you have love for one another."

(4) In this hour of fellowship, Jesus, Who had hitherto referred to Himself as the Son of Man, made it quite clear in a reply to Philip, that He had a special relationship to the Father. He replied, as an Avatar might well have done, "Have I been with you so long, and yet you do not know Me, Philip? He who has seen Me has seen the Father ... Believe Me, that I am in the Father, and the Father in Me ..."

(5) He spoke to them of the importance of *trusting* Him. His frequently used term is translated "abiding in" Him. "If you abide in Me, and My words abide in you, ask whatever you will and it shall be done for you ... As the Father has loved Me, so have I loved you; abide in My love. If you keep My commandments you will abide in My love ... This is my commandment, that you love one another, as I have loved you."

(6) He prophesied for them hatred and persecution by the world, and that they would be driven from their synagogues. "Indeed the hour is coming when whoever kills you will think that he is offering service to God." Blood, sweat, toil, and tears, were forecast as their lot, but He reminded them that the servant is not greater than His Master. Since the world had treated Him in this way, they must expect it also. "In the world you will have tribulation" He said, "but be of good cheer, I have overcome the world."

(7) He reminded them that they had infinite resources to draw upon. "Truly, truly, I say unto you, if you ask anything of the Father, He will give it to you in My Name. Hitherto you have asked nothing in My Name: ask and you will receive, that your joy may be full."

(8) He promised them special Help from the Father, – a Counsellor and Guide, the Holy Spirit, – Who would interpret and explain His teachings to them and "bring to your remembrance all that I have said to you."

(9) Finally, He blessed them with that most precious gift of His own peace. These words have echoed in loving and devout hearts for two thousand years. "Peace I leave with you; My peace I give unto you; not as the world gives, give I unto you.

Let not your heart be troubled, neither let it be afraid."
He told them that He was not of this world; that He was returning to His Father's Kingdom, and that He was going ahead
to prepare the way for them. Was there ever in history, such a
farewell as this? Its crown is the prayer of Jesus to His Heavenly
Father, recorded in the 17th chapter of St John. It breathes
Love, it speaks Love, it is Love. It should be read in silence
and meditated upon in private. Did they understand Him then?
Were their eyes wet with tears as they walked with Him across
the Kedron valley to the garden of betrayal?

> King ever glorious!
> > The dews of death are gath'ring round Thee;
> > Upon the cross Thy foes have bound Thee
> Thy strength is gone.
>
> Not in Majesty
> > Robed in Heaven's supremest splendour
> > But in weakness and surrender
> Thou hangest here.
>
> Who can be like Thee?
> > Pilate high in Zion dwelling,
> > Rome with arms the world compelling,
> Proud though they be?
>
> Thou art sublime;
> > Far more awful in Thy weakness,
> > More than kingly in Thy meekness,
> Thou Son of God.
>
> Glory and honour:
> > Let the world divide and take them;
> > Crown its monarchs and unmake them;
> But Thou wilt reign.
>
> Here in abasement;
> > Crownless, poor, disrobed, and bleeding,
> > There in glory interceding,
> Thou art the King! Thou art the King!

3/25